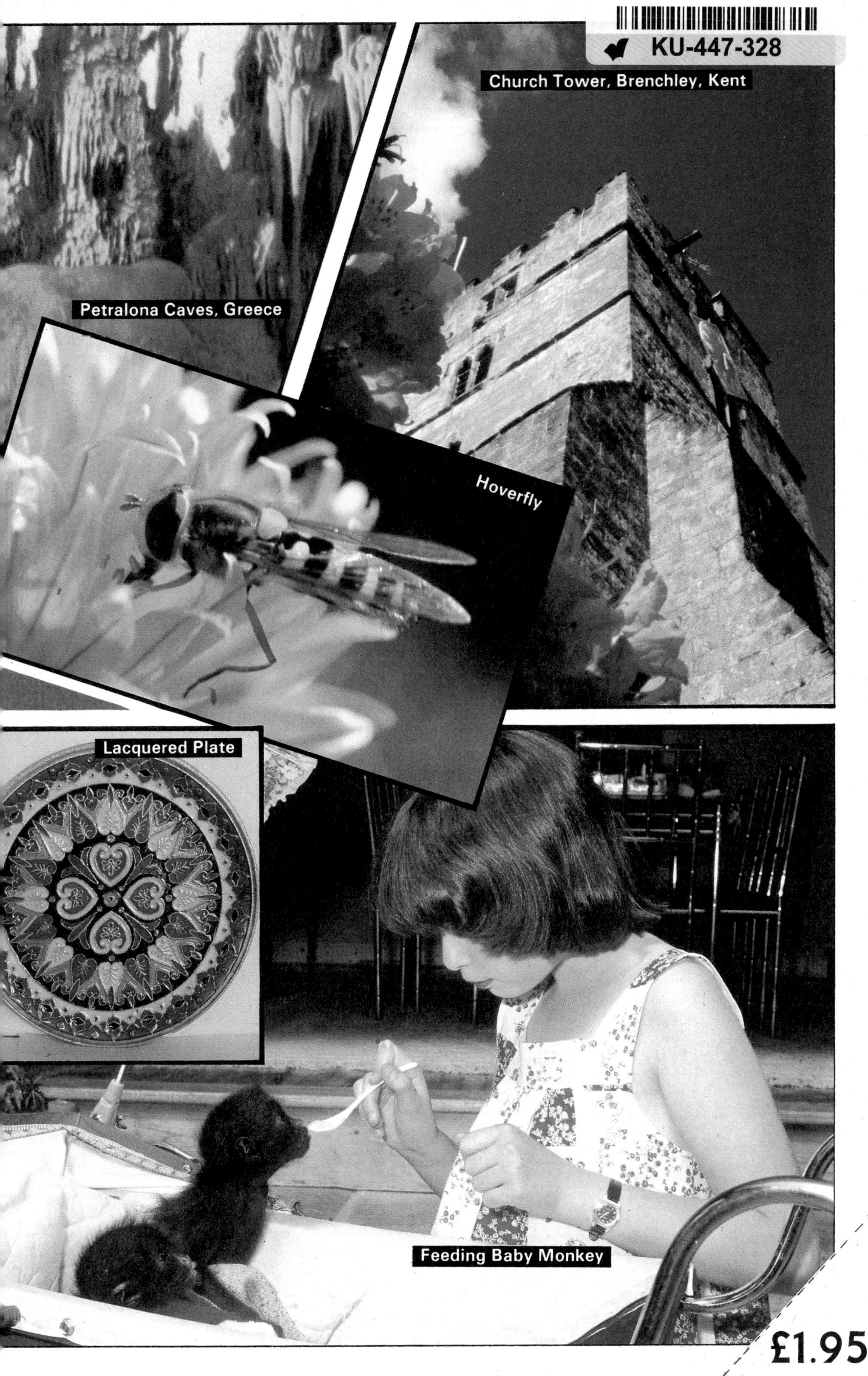
KU-447-328
Church Tower, Brenchley, Kent
Petralona Caves, Greece
Hoverfly
Lacquered Plate
Feeding Baby Monkey
£1.95

Printed and Published in Great Britain by D. C. Thomson & Co., Ltd., 185 Fleet Street, London, EC4A 2HS. 
ISBN 0 85116 274 6

Silver Star
It's no good, Mr Davies—Star won't let me saddle him!
Only Megan could ride him, Jerry, before she had her fall.
EVAN DAVIES, owner of a riding stable in Wales, had a daughter, Megan, who had lain in a coma for almost a year. He also had an unrideable horse called Silver Star.
But the story really began many, many miles away, a year earlier.
Emergency! Captain Zoros' scouting ship is out of control! It is on a collision course for the planet called Earth!
Set course for the planet! We must rescue him!
On that same day—
Get off that mare! Dad, I told you not to let any of these beginners ride Blaze!
Megan always got her way.
These fools can ruin a good horse in weeks!
Very well, Megan. We'll try one of the older mares.
That same evening, a blaze of light lit the stable yard.

What was that?
A meteorite, I think! Better call the vet! Royal Silver's in foal and the shock may have upset her!
The vet came quickly, and Royal Silver's foal was delivered prematurely.
Premature foals are usually weak for some time, but this one's a fighter.
I want him, Dad! I shall call him Silver Star, after the meteorite!
Over the next four months, Silver Star made amazing progress.
I never saw a foal grow this fast, Miss Megan!
He's special, Jerry. Just make sure none of those novices gets to ride him!
Meanwhile, Megan's father had received a report on the strange meteorite.
It seems the meteorite was hollow, Megan. There may have been something inside it—but no one knows what.
Before long, Megan was riding Silver Star. He was only months old, yet he looked like a two-year-old.
He's magnificent, Jerry!
There's something not right about that horse . . . something in the way he looks at you. He's just too intelligent!

What do you know, Jerry Coates? Even when you were a jockey you were no good! Dad only keeps you on out of sympathy! Go, Star!
That girl is riding for a fall. She's too proud.
Come on, Star! Let's show the beginners some real riding!
You'll never learn to ride, kids! You haven't got it in you!
Megan!

This is all I need—Star, and the open countryside!
But Megan was no entirely alone.
We have detected Captain Zoros. His life-force has adopted an Earth-creature.
Close in on him.
Later—
Have you seen Megan? It's getting late.
Not since this afternoon, Mr Davies.
We'd better go and see if we can find her.
Megan was miles away— and terrified.
That is the creature. It is very odd. Six legs and two heads.
Transport it up.
Within a few moments—
This is not one creature but two. One is the dominant species, the other a mere beast of burden.

What will we do now?
Extract Captain Zoros' life-force from the creatures, and return their own personalities. Then put them back on the planet's surface.
Hours later—
There's something over there, Jerry!
Jerry—come quickly! It's Megan and she seems to be in a coma! She must have fallen!
But the aliens had made a mistake when returning the Earthlings' life forces to their bodies.
Take Star back to the stables, Jerry! I'll look after Megan!
Dad! It's me, Megan! Can't you hear me?
Megan Davies had loved horses more than she had loved people, but now she was trapped inside the body of Silver Star—with no chance of escape!
So, almost a year later—
It's a spirited horse, all right!
Aye, as spirited as Megan was herself—before her fall.
It was a year to the day before the aliens, accidentally discovering the mistake they had made, returned to put things right . . . and it was a completely different, kind and considerate Megan who then came back to normal life. She couldn't tell anyone why she had changed. Who would have believed her?
THE END.

# SOME OF HER BEST FRIENDS HAVE FEATHERS!

Kestrel Becky is a film star. She appeared in " Tarka the Otter " and the TV series, " Brandon Chase ".

**Anna Williams works at the Hawk Conservancy, near Andover. She helps to look after hawks, owls, falcons, vultures and kites.**

This barn owl is a great favourite at the Hawk Conservancy.

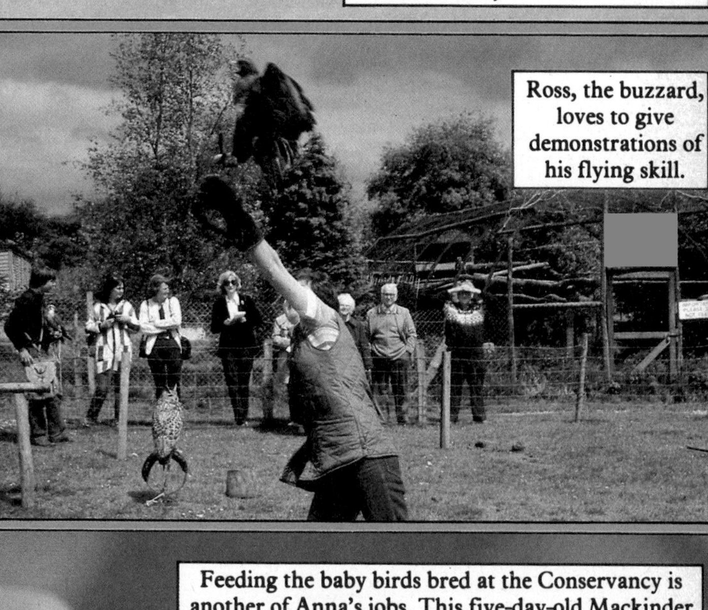

Ross, the buzzard, loves to give demonstrations of his flying skill.

Feeding the baby birds bred at the Conservancy is another of Anna's jobs. This five-day-old Mackinder eagle owl looks as if it is enjoying its dinner.

These two European eagle owls are the first of their species to be born at the Conservancy.

Whoops! Some of the older youngsters can prove a handful, like this rare Harris hawk.

Anna becomes a shopkeeper when visitors want a memento of their visit.

Gonzo shows off his wingspan. This vulture weighs 23 kilos and must be treated with respect.

Anna loves the peacocks that roam around the Conservancy. " But at night," she says, " when they call to one another, it's the eeriest sound you can imagine."

At the end of her working day, Anna goes home and feeds her own animals. They include six rabbits, two dogs, four cats and her horses—Mandy, Whizzy, Gee and Willie.

BOBBY DAZZLER
Look at this, Mike! A model 'plane contest!
MODEL AEROPLANE BUILDING *** COMPETITION ***
FIRST XV RUGBY TEAM
To be judged next Saturday by Mark Steadman, the famous Westbury old boy! And the first prize is a camera, Don!
I think I'll have a try at that myself.
BOBBY DAZZLER was the only girl at Westbury Boarding School for Boys, where her mother was matron. Two other third-formers, Mike Norton and Don Carter, were her great admirers—and rivals too! One morning—
'Plane modelling is for boys. You stick to feminine pastimes, Bobby, like flower-arranging!
Huh! I'll show you!
Think what fools we'd look if Bobby won! She's better than lots of boys at all sorts of things!
When it comes to designing a 'plane, I bet you she won't know where to start!

But, a few days later, in the hobbies room—
It seems Bobby has a flair for modelling after all!
We'll be the laughing stock of the school if she beats us in this contest!
Then Bobby's mother arrived—
Don't you think you ought to be putting in some music practice, Bobby? Your exam's on Friday.
You're right, Mum, worse luck. I'd better leave this model for now.
We must stop her winning that contest, Mike!
Dead right! What's needed is a spot of sabotage. Just wait till she goes out of the room . . .
Hey, Bobby! Where are you taking that?
To lock it in Mum's cupboard till Saturday morning. I've a hunch there are one or two jokers around this place!
After breakfast on Saturday morning—
I've promised Beaky I'll make a flower display for the school hall. Then I must work hard on my'plane model for the rest of the morning.

I guess there's no stopping her now, Mike!
I haven't given up yet! At all costs we must keep her away from that'plane of hers . . .

. . . and here's how we'll do it!
No one's likely to come near here on a Saturday. We'll leave her to cool her heels for an hour or two.
Like we said, Bobby—you stick to flower arranging!
They've locked me in! Of all the grotty tricks! Looks like I don't stand a chance of winning that camera now!

But wait . . . There could be a way! I even brought some wire with me to use for the floral arrangement.

At a quarter to twelve—
Bobby! Do you mean to say you've been locked in here all morning? You'll never finish that model 'plane you've been working on!
Never mind that, Mum! Come and take a look at this!

That afternoon, the famous old boy announced the winner of the contest.
An interesting selection of entries—but the prize must undoubtedly go to the maker of this delightful and imaginative model. Step forward, Roberta Dazzler.
BOBBY?
It—it's unbelievable! She made a model 'plane out of those FLOWERS!
I went by their suggestion and stuck to flower arranging—and now the camera's mine because of it!
THE END

# Wedding Belle

Clare is to be a bridesmaid. After all the fittings and alterations, the dress is ready. Everyone admires her.

Having your hair in rollers can be a drag—but today Clare doesn't mind, for it's a big occasion.

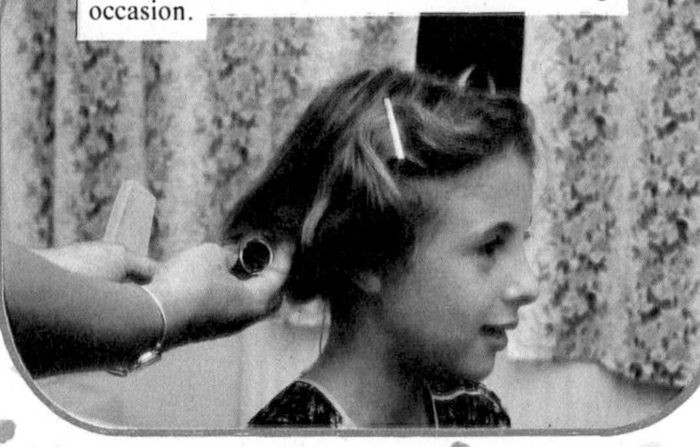

Next comes the nail-biting bit! The bride and bridesmaids are about to enter the church.

Now the church service is coming to an end. The bride and groom are man and wife.

Confetti can be a problem if you have long hair! Never mind, it's worth it.

Here's a miniature bridesmaid! Clare shows a doll wearing a replica of her own dress.

To help her remember the occasion, the bride has given Clare a pendant necklace—but Clare won't need much reminding of her big day!

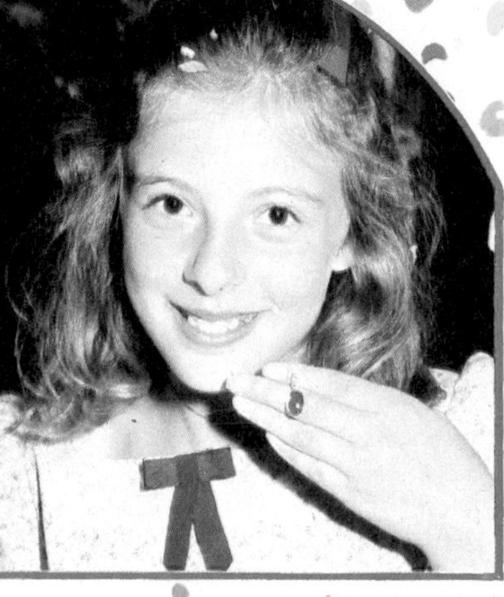

Clare joins the happy couple by the wedding cake.

ANN PELHAM lived with her brilliant but hard-up uncle, who was an nventor. One day he ushered her xcitedly down some dusty steps and nto the cellars of their rambling Victorian house.
THE TIME MACHINE
This is it, Ann—my greatest invention! It'll make our fortunes!
Yes, Uncle Jack! I'll believe it when I see it!
Here it is, my dear! A time machine!
YEAR
DURATION
LOCATION
A time machine? You get nuttier every day, Uncle Jack! If I don't fetch your pension, there'll be no meal tonight!
In town, a newspaper headline caught Ann's eye.
PAINTING FETCHES £1MILLION
A million pounds! Just for a picture! And we're struggling on Uncle's pension!

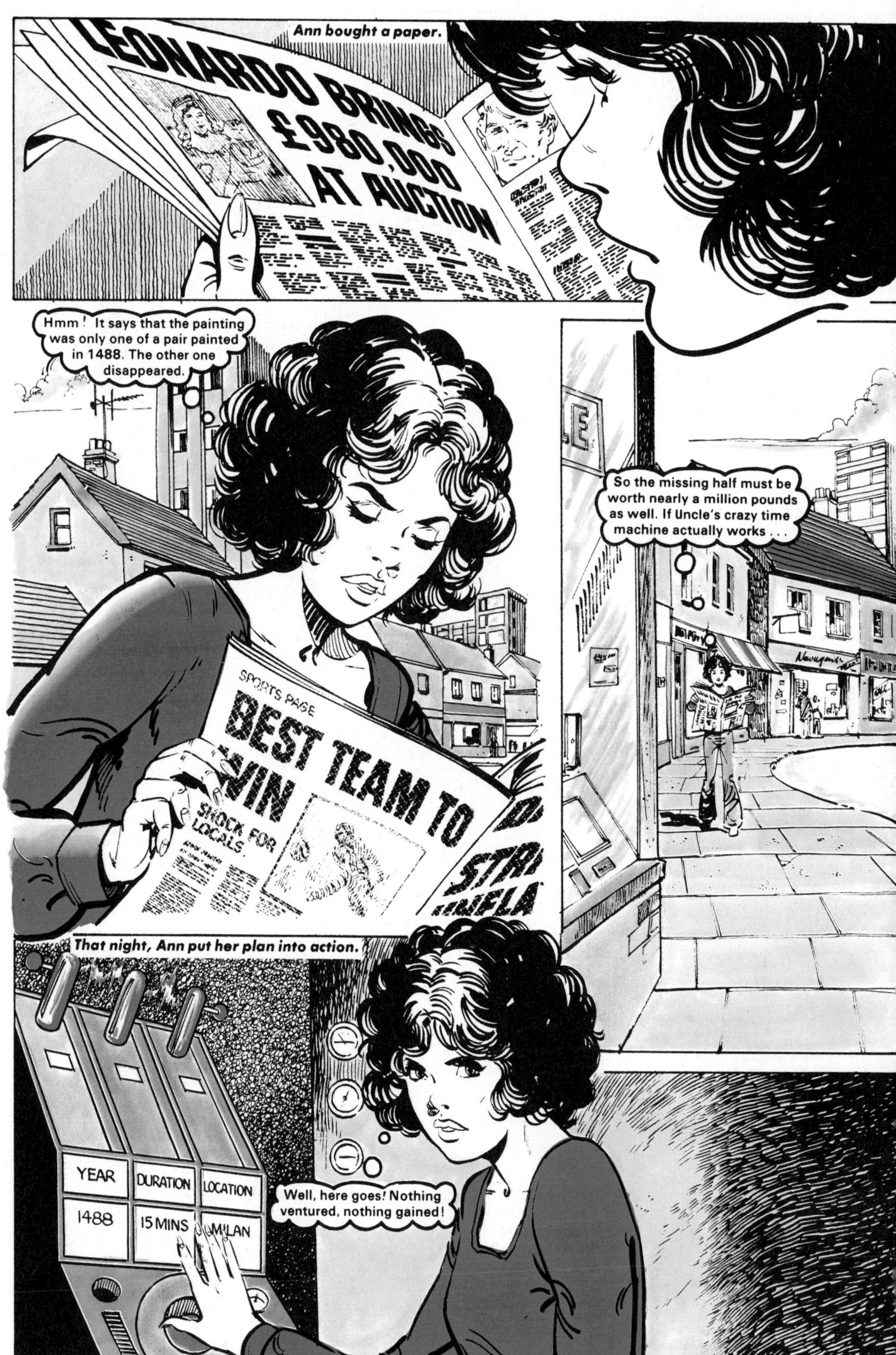
Ann bought a paper.
LEONARDO BRINGS £980,000 AT AUCTION
Hmm! It says that the painting was only one of a pair painted in 1488. The other one disappeared.
SPORTS PAGE
BEST TEAM TO WIN
SHOCK FOR LOCALS.
So the missing half must be worth nearly a million pounds as well. If Uncle's crazy time machine actually works . . .
That night, Ann put her plan into action.
YEAR
DURATION
LOCATION
1488
15 MINS
MILAN
Well, here goes! Nothing ventured, nothing gained!

Aaaaagh! He's really done it! It works!
1934
1488
1512
1579
1656
1705
1772
Within a few moments, Ann found herself in Leonardo's studio in Milan, 1488.
Yow! This floor's hard!
Signorina?
That's it! The missing painting!
I'd like to—er—buy that painting. Please!
Non capisco, signorina!
Of course, he doesn't speak English! I'll have to use sign language to offer my bracelet in exchange for the picture.
The deal was quickly done.
Any moment now, I'll be popping back to the nineteen-eighties!
Goodbye, Mr Leonardo!
Arrivederla, signorina, e grazie!

Seconds later, Ann was back in her own time.
Who's there? What's going on?
It's Uncle Jack! I must hide the picture!
Ann! What are you doing down here in the middle of the night?
I—I was wondering if your new invention actually works.
I haven't tested it yet. You must promise me, Ann, never to reveal its existence to anybody! Well?
All right, I promise.
Next day, Ann's uncle had to go out.
Hello! Is that the auctioneers? I think I've discovered the lost Leonardo!
What? I'll be round right away!

Ann was in for a disappointment.
It's brilliant! Absolutely superb—but it's obviously a fake. The paint is much too fresh.
Oh, but I know . . . I mean, are you sure?

Anyway, Leonardo sold the painting in return for a silver trinket in 1488. It's probably been destroyed by now. I'll give you fifty pounds . . . curiosity value.
A silver trinket?

I'll be off, then. Goodbye!
What? Oh, yes, all right.

That's how the picture disappeared! Because *I* went back and swopped it for my bracelet! If I hadn't done that, it wouldn't have been lost!
Still, at least I have enough to buy myself a new bracelet—and a present for Uncle Jack!
THE END.

YOU MIGHT THINK THAT AN EGGSHELL IS TOO FRAGILE FOR MAKING JEWELLERY, BUT FOLLOW THE INSTRUCTIONS AND YOU'LL BE SURPRISED HOW STRONG AND ATTRACTIVE IT IS.

FIRST, CUT THE TOP FROM AN EGGSHELL, MAKING THE EDGE AS SMOOTH AS POSSIBLE BY NIBBLING ROUND WITH NAIL SCISSORS. THEN CUT A CARD DISC, ROUGHLY 15 MM. LARGER IN DIAMETER THAN YOUR SHELL, AND GLUE TOGETHER, AS YOU SEE BELOW.

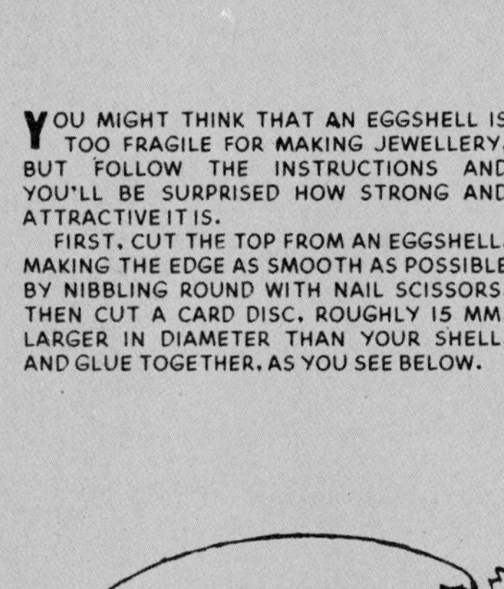

# MAKE THIS EGGSHELL CAMEO

ACTUAL SIZE

DECORATE AS YOU SEE HERE, WITH A PICTURE GLUED ON THE SHELL, THE CARD PAINTED BLACK, OR WHATEVER, AND THE WHOLE PAINTED OVER WITH CLEAR VARNISH.

GLUE LUREX THREAD, GOLD FINGERING, OR SIMILAR STRING TRIMMING ROUND THE SHELL AND THE EDGE OF THE CARD, THEN A WAVY LINE IN BETWEEN.

HANG YOUR CAMEO ON COLOURED SILK, AND IT'S COMPLETE.

NOTE: IF YOUR CHOSEN PICTURE IS ON THICK PAPER, PEEL THE BACKING OFF, THEN SOAK IN WATER BEFORE GLUING, SO THAT IT WILL TAKE UP THE CURVED SHAPE OF THE EGGSHELL.

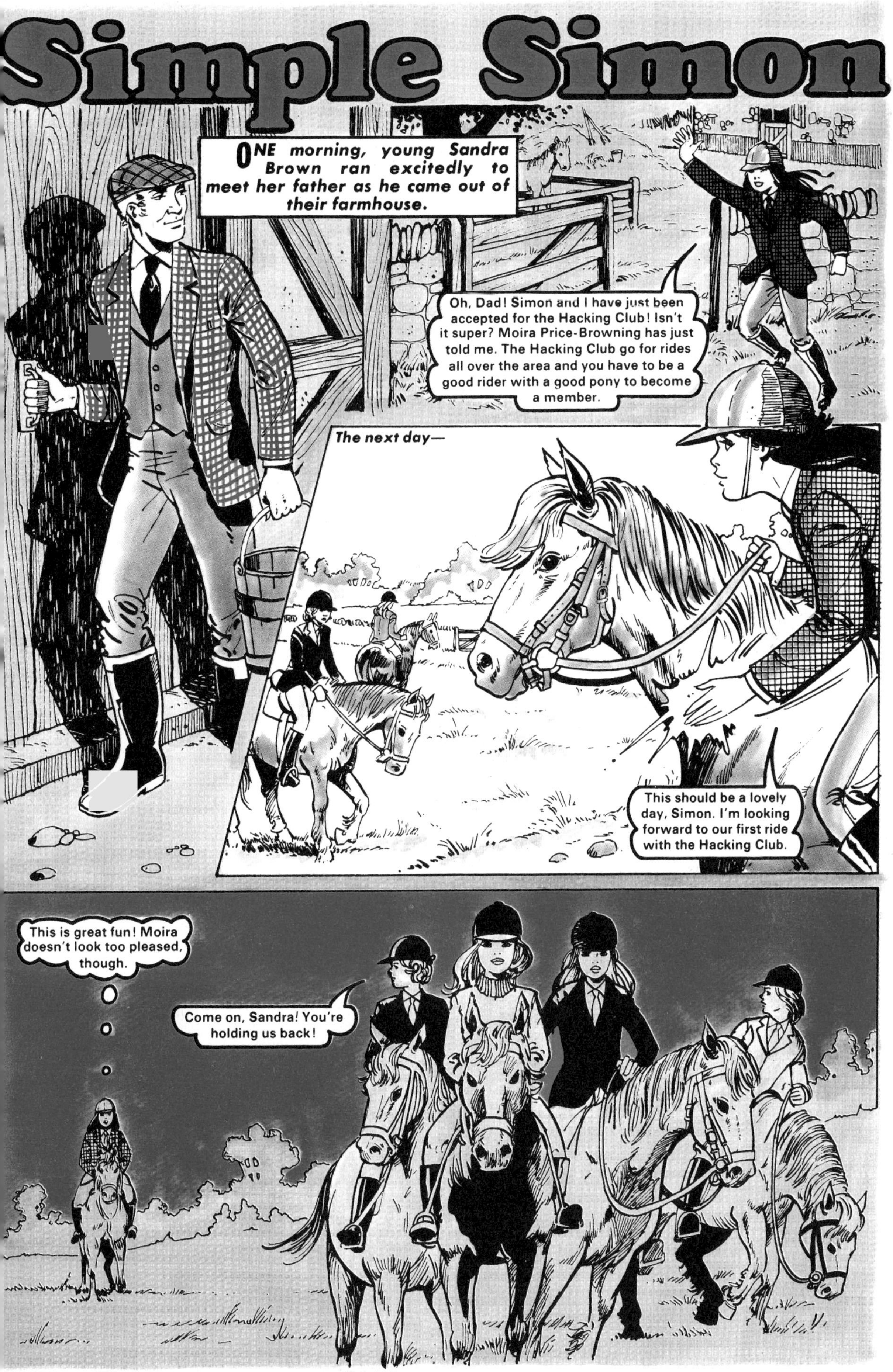

# Simple Simon

**ONE morning, young Sandra Brown ran excitedly to meet her father as he came out of their farmhouse.**

Oh, Dad! Simon and I have just been accepted for the Hacking Club! Isn't it super? Moira Price-Browning has just told me. The Hacking Club go for rides all over the area and you have to be a good rider with a good pony to become a member.

*The next day—*

This should be a lovely day, Simon. I'm looking forward to our first ride with the Hacking Club.

This is great fun! Moira doesn't look too pleased, though.

Come on, Sandra! You're holding us back!

Two or three weeks passed and Sandra was enjoying her outings with the Hacking Club. Then, one morning—
Moira Price-Browning! What can she want?
I've been asked to tell you that the club has voted you out. You keep trailing behind the rest of us. Frankly, that pony of yours is not up to our standard. You should call him " Simple Simon "!
Oh, Simon, what a disappointment! But I'd rather have you, any day, than any of their ponies, no matter how fast they are.
Next day—
It's a nice day. We'll go for a ride on our own, Simon. Who needs the Hacking Club?
Later—
Help! Help!
What's wrong, Moira?
It's Prince! He's trapped in the boggy ground near the river! The more he struggles, the deeper he sinks!
Stay here! Try to calm him down, Moira! I'm off to get my dad!

Ten minutes later—
Oh, thank goodness you've come! Prince is sinking deeper!
After two unsuccessful attempts, Sandra's father managed to lasso the struggling pony.
As soon as I've tied this to his saddle, you start leading
OK, Dad!
Good boy, Simon! Come on! You can do it!
Simon gradually guided and pulled Prince to safety.
Well done, Simon! You proved you're not simple!
Next day, Moira came to see Sandra.
Sandra, I've come to say how grateful I am to you and Simon,and to say we've had a unanimous vote at the club to welcome you and Simon back—if you want to come, that is.
Oh, yes—Simon and I would love to join again!
THE END

# LOTS TO DO

## CROSSWORDS

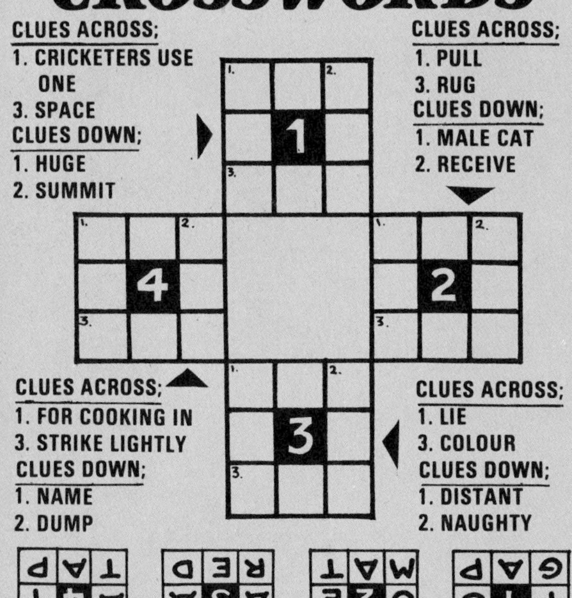

**1**
CLUES ACROSS;
1. CRICKETERS USE ONE
3. SPACE

CLUES DOWN;
1. HUGE
2. SUMMIT

**2**
CLUES ACROSS;
1. PULL
3. RUG

CLUES DOWN;
1. MALE CAT
2. RECEIVE

**3**
CLUES ACROSS;
1. LIE
3. COLOUR

CLUES DOWN;
1. DISTANT
2. NAUGHTY

**4**
CLUES ACROSS;
1. FOR COOKING IN
3. STRIKE LIGHTLY

CLUES DOWN;
1. NAME
2. DUMP

BAT / I 1 O / GAP

TUG / O 2 E / MAT

FIB / A 3 A / RED

POT / A 4 I / TAP

## FAMOUS LANDMARKS

DO YOU RECOGNISE THEM?

A.

B.

C.

D.

ANSWERS—A. EIFFEL TOWER B. BIG BEN C. STATUE OF LIBERTY D. SYDNEY OPERA HOUSE

## WHO ARE THEY ?

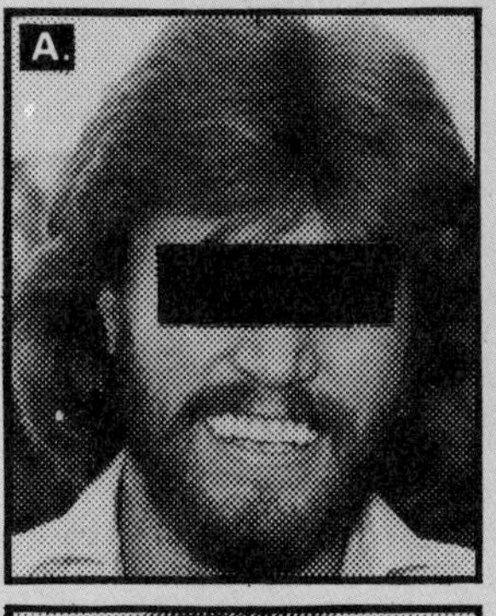
A.

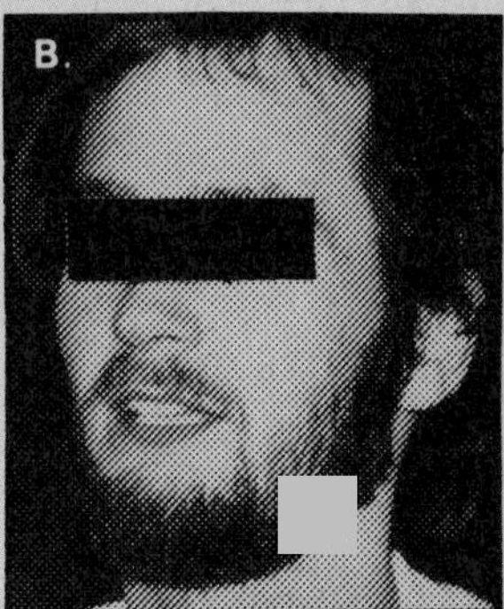
B.

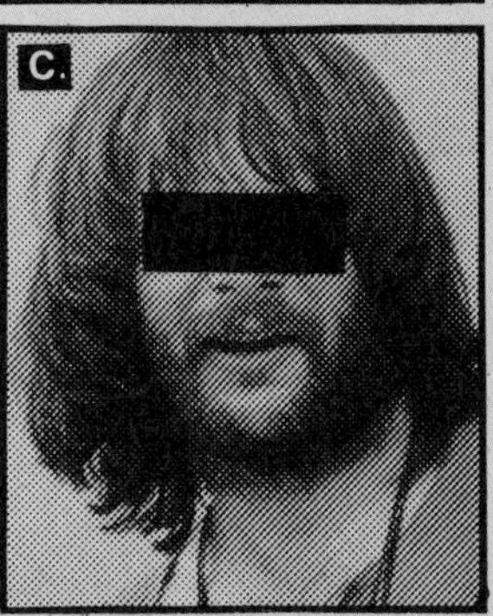
C.

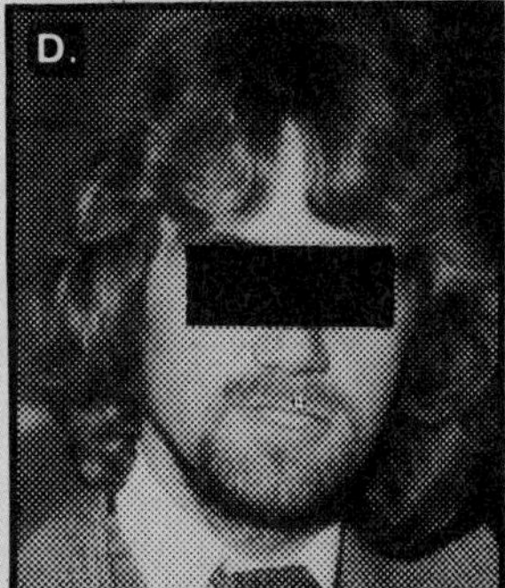
D.

ANSWERS—A. BARRY GIBB B. KENNY EVERETT C. BILL ODDIE D. NOEL EDMONDS

## MAZES

START

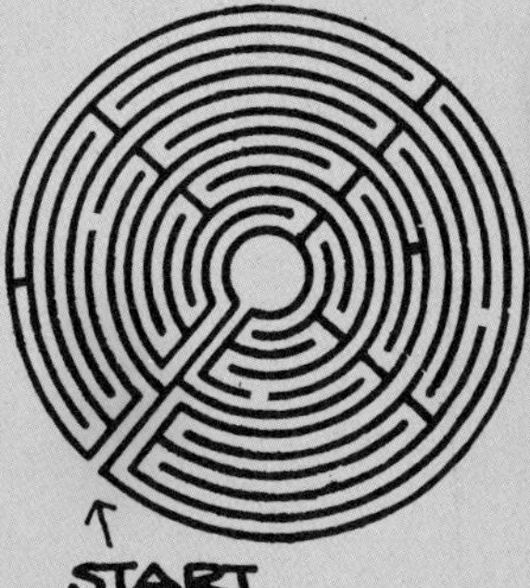
START

START

START

# Schoolgirl Vet

KAY BURROWS loved all animals and hoped one day to become a vet like her brother, David.
There's Constable Clark exercising Rex. I must go and say hello.
POLICE
Rex loves this game. I bet he'd keep it up all day.
He's trained to bring things to me, but not to let anyone else take anything from him. He'd attack them if they tried. That's why I bring him here only when it's quiet.
But the beach wasn't as deserted as the constable had thought.
What a lovely dog!
No! Stop!
Sorry if I scared you. He's trained to be suspicious of anyone who offers him something. It could be a crook, trying to poison him, you see.

That evening, when Kay's brother arrived home—
What a day! I reckon I've earned a chance to put my feet up.
I'm afraid you won't get a chance yet, David. Here comes Constable Clark.
POLICE
I'm sorry to disturb you this late, Mr Burrows, but I didn't think this could wait until morning. Rex seems to have something seriously wrong with him.
Bring him into the surgery.
Soon—
He's been poisoned!
Poisoned? You mean some thug has done it deliberately to get him out of the way?
But you *can* save him?
Perhaps. I've got to find out what the poison is before I can start treating it.
What baffles me is how anyone could have tricked Rex. He's so smart that he'd refuse anything unless I gave it to him.
I wonder . . .
Mum, please drive me down to the sea-front gardens. It's urgent.
Very well, Kay. I'll just turn off the cooker.

*Meanwhile, in the small surgery —*

Rex is in a bad way, Mr Burrows.

I'm doing my best, Constable Clark.

*David was still baffled when Kay returned.*

How's it going?

Nothing to smile at! I'm beginning to think I've got it all wrong. I must have missed something.

When Constable Clark said Rex was too well trained to take anything from strangers, I began to wonder whether it could be anything he had taken from the constable—and I think it was this piece of wood he was fetching!

Laburnum—and he's almost made a meal of it! Well done, Kay!

It's poisonous? I had no idea!

I can save Rex, but he's going to need careful nursing. We'll have to keep him here until he's well.

Thanks! Thanks a lot, Mr Burrows!

A few days later—
Rex is fine now.
Thanks, Kay. You and your brother have done a grand job.
POLI

*As Constable Clark drove back to the police station with Rex—*

PETROL
POLICE
There's no driver in the cab! The handbrake must have failed! I've got to do something, or there'll be a terrible crash!

Hup, boy!

*As the tanker's brakes had failed, Constable Clark could only guide the runaway vehicle on to some waste ground.*

He risked his own neck to save a lot of people from being killed! We've got to help him!

Watch it! The tanker may blow up at any second!

Within minutes someone had alerted the police and fire brigade.
We've got to pull Clark clear before the tanker explodes!
GRRR!
The dog won't let us near him! It'll tear us to pieces!

David, giving Kay a lift to school, arrived on the scene.
The dog has been trained to defend Clark and won't let anyone near! We've no choice but to shoot it!
Oh, no!

Let me see what I can do.
It's very risky, miss.
I think it's worth a try. Kay has spent a lot of time with the dog— but, at the first sign of danger, we'll have to shoot.
Kay began to walk slowly and fearlessly towards Rex.
This isn't going to work! Rex is getting ready to spring!
Kay! Run!
No! Don't fire!
Good boy, Rex. Come on, we're going to help your master.
You can come and fetch Constable Clark now. Rex understands.
Within a few days Rex and Constable Clark were back on duty.
It's great to see you both around again.
Neither of us might be here, but for you— and I guess Rex knows that as well as I do.
THE END

*Picnics; walks, school trips; the garden—remember THIS summer in winter, when the winds blow cold, with pretty flower calendars or pictures made very simply. In summer, press some flowers or leaves between layers of blotting paper between flat boards piled high with heavy bricks (An old-fashioned trouser press is ideal if you can lay your hands on one.)*

*In winter, lay a dried flower on a piece of very firm cardboard, delicately coloured if possible. Cover entire card and flower with thin plastic film used for wrapping food. This holds the flower firmly in place. Attach a ribbon at top for pinning on wall and add a little date calendar if you wish. Now you can remember this summer beautifully!*

## THROW A MOOD DICE

*These easily-made, colourful dice make a fun addition to your bedroom or desk, or novel gifts.*

*Trace the shape on the page, then trace it onto card. Cut along solid lines on card then fold along dotted lines. Fold all flaps in. Stick the outside of Flap 'A' to outside of Flap 'B'. Now fold in 'C' flaps and stick to the outside of the 'D' flaps. Similarly, stick the 'E' flaps to the 'F' flaps. Now you should have one cube. Draw and colour your moods on each face—then let the world know how you feel today!*

*To make an instant example of these dice, cut out the specimen on this page.*

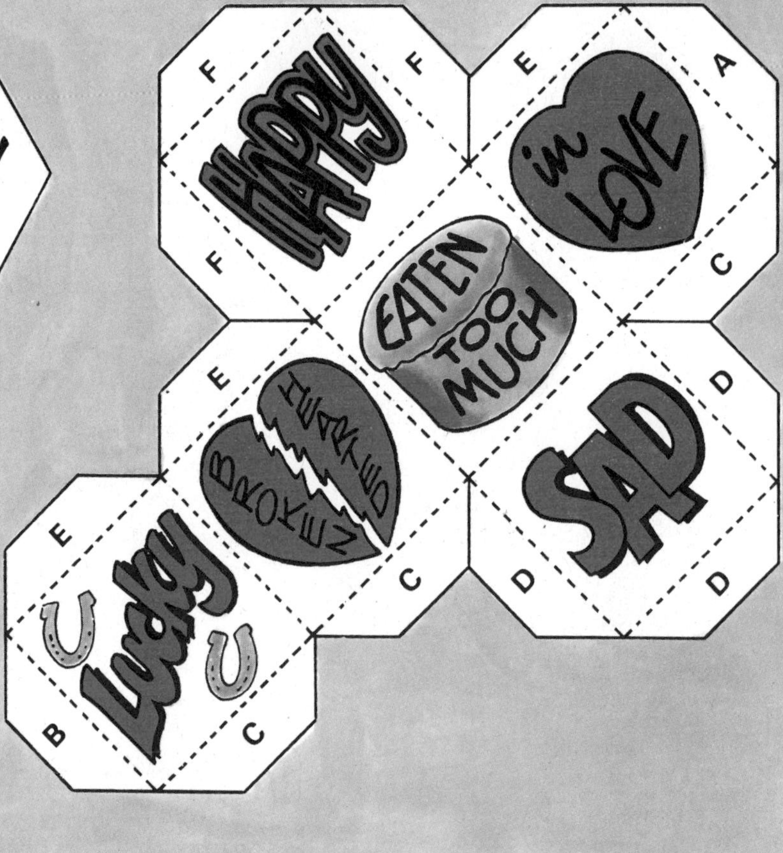

# A Year And A Day

Norfolk, England, June 1738, and Squire Jonas Welkin and his new bride, Althea, were returning to their remote estate in the fens.

Eeeeaah!

I told you to drive slower, coachman! We've hit old Gammer Woodthorpe....the one they call the witch!

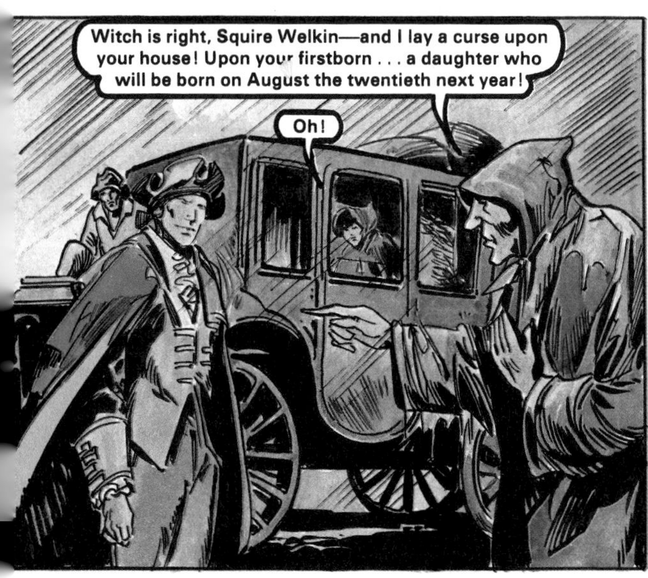

Witch is right, Squire Welkin—and I lay a curse upon your house! Upon your firstborn . . . a daughter who will be born on August the twentieth next year!
Oh!

I give the child a year and a day for each member of my coven! After thirteen years and thirteen days, the Angel of Death will come for her—and he cannot return empty handed! September the third, 1752, he takes her!

As if by magic, the old crone vanished.
Jonas! She frightens me!
Pay no attention, my love. She's just a poor, mad old woman. Drive on, coachman.

On the 20th August, 1739, just after midnight, Alona Welkin was born.
Jonas, I keep thinking about that old woman's curse. She was right about the birthdate, after all.
No harm shall come to our daughter, my sweet. I swear it!

Alona grew up with few friends from the village, but she did have a younger brother and sister.
Alona is ten tomorrow. How the years fly!
The children play well together, Jonas.

A tutor from the nearest town taught Alona her lessons.
Excellent, Alona!

The years passed quickly and soon it was Alona's thirteenth birthday
A party? That would be wonderful!
All the children from the village will be invited.

The 20th of August, 1752, dawned bright and clear, and the party went well . . . at first.
Bravo! Well found!
Jonas, look at the clouds. I think there's going to be a storm.

And, suddenly—
Thirteen years and thirteen days! Did you think I would forget? The thirteen years are up today!
Jonas!

In thirteen days the Angel of Death will come for her! The third of September! Ha ha ha!
Get out of here, you old hag!

As the fateful day approached, tension mounted.
I tell you that woman has no power over life and death! It's superstitious nonsense!
Nevertheless, I shall stay by Alona's side tonight!

That night, as midnight approached—
Mother! What's that noise? It sounded like horse's hooves downstairs!
Wait here, Alona! I shall go and see!

*Althea went on to the landing, and—*

It's the Angel of Death!

I seek Alona Welkin, of this house.

*At that moment, the clock struck midnight, and—*

Mother . . . the storm just suddenly stopped!

Who spoke from the hall?

The Angel of Death! He came for Alona!

But he did not take her! Heaven be praised!
He just vanished, at the moment the new day began!

Next morning, the tutor had some news.
Morning, Jonas. Heard the news? The old witch Gammer Woodthorpe has disappeared . . . carried off screaming in the night, so the locals say.

he Squire took the tutor in to his study.
Haven't you adjusted your diary, Jonas?
Adjusted it? What do you mean?

You're so isolated here! You really should keep up with the news! The calendar changes today!
What? I don't understand!

The old Roman calendar didn't count its leap-years properly. The government is adopting the Gregorian calendar from today. It's not the third . . . it's the fourteenth!
So?
The old calendar was eleven days out, so eleven days have been dropped.
So the second of September, 1752, is followed by the fourteenth of September, 1752?

The curse was for September the third this year—but there has been no September the third!
That's why the Angel of Death disappeared at midnight! And he couldn't go back empty-handed—so he took the old woman!
THE END

# A 'Judy' Cake

**Ingredients for the cake:—**
150 g. (6 oz.) self-raising flour. Three size-2 eggs
150 g. (6 oz.) soft margarine.
150 g. (6 oz.) caster sugar.

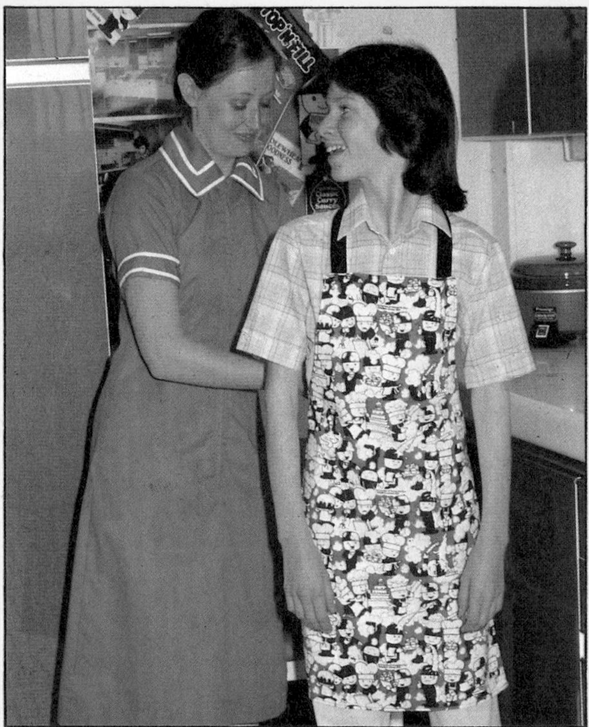

**1.** Thirteen-year-old Leisa Banks is keen on baking, so we took her along to help us show you, step by step, how to make our "Judy" cake. When Leisa arrived at the New Malden Homepride Kitchen, she was greeted by Allyson Birch, the home economist who worked out the recipe for our "Judy" cake. If you are trying out the recipe, remember to use your apron. Also, ask a grown-up to light the oven, if it's a gas one—and don't bake when you are in the house alone.

**2.** Leisa collected all the ingredients together. Allyson had already pre-heated the oven to the temperature of 180 deg. C., 350 deg. F., Gas Mark 4.

3. You should also prepare the baking tins before you start to make the cake. You need two 22 cm. (8½ in.) sandwich tins. Draw round the tins on greaseproof paper, cut out the two circles to fit inside the bottom of the tins, then grease each tin lightly. Leisa is using oil and a small brush. It is quick and simple to use, but you can also use butter or soft margarine.

**4.** Put all the ingredients for the cake into a large mixing bowl and beat for three minutes, by which time the mixture should be pale and creamy, showing that it is ready. Divide the mixture into your two ready-prepared tins and spread it evenly.

**5.** If you are baking for the first time, remember to ask an adult to help you put the sponges in the oven. The sponges will take between 25 and 30 minutes to bake. They will be golden brown and firm to the touch when they are ready. Leave them in the tins for five minutes, then gently turn them out onto a wire tray and leave them to cool. Remove the paper from the bottom of each layer.

**6.** Here are the sponges baked and ready for decorating.

# for Christmas

**Ingredients for the lemon butter icing:—**
200 g. (8 oz.) icing sugar. 100 g. (4 oz.) butter, softened.
Grated rind and juice of one small lemon.
A few drops of yellow food colouring.

**Ingredients for decoration:—**
Orange-coloured sweets, or small jelly diamonds.
Orange and lemon jelly slices.
Yellow ribbon.

7. To make the lemon butter icing, sift he icing sugar into a bowl, grate he rind and squeeze the juice from the emon, add the butter to the icing sugar and beat until it is well-blended and creamy. Now put in the lemon rind, juice and just three or four drops of colouring— no more. Mix the icing thoroughly.

**8.** Place one layer of sponge on a 25 cm. (10 in.) round cake board, or plate, and spread with one third of the lemon icing. Put three large spoonfuls of the remaining icing in a piping bag fitted with a small star nozzle. Place the second sponge on top of the first and spread the remaining icing on the top. If you want to make a swirling pattern, draw the knife backwards and forwards across the cake.

**9.** If you haven't piped stars before, practise round a plate. Allyson showed us this tip and it took Leisa only a few minutes to make the stars look nice. Now, pipe the small stars round the edge of the cake itself.

**10.** Make the word " JUDY " with orange sweets, or jelly diamonds, on the top of the cake, and place orange and lemon jelly slices around the edge.

**11.** For a very special occasion, decorate the cake with a ribbon. Doesn't the cake look super?

**12.** And it tastes just as good as it looks!

# A FAST LEARNER

**MARIE REAGAN and her family had always been travelling folk. One day, Marie was told she would have to go to school.**

I don't mind school, so long as I can take Poll with me.
A parrot? Well, I don't really think . . .

But Marie wouldn't be parted from her beloved pet.
Look at her, Carol! Do you suppose she's come to tell our fortunes?
Don't get too close, Bev. You might catch something!

This must be a fine type of school, if that's the best you can do in the way of a welcome!
It *was* until you arrived! Listen, we don't want your sort here, so just keep out of the way!

Although Marie had not been to school often, she was bright.
I can read and write, and do sums as well. My dad taught me. Give me books, sir. I'm a fast learner.
Yes, well, start by putting your—er—parrot in the locker-room.

lessons started—
use me askin', sir, but what would a square root be? Some kind o' vegetable?
No, not quite. But don't worry about it, Marie. I'll give you some books to help you catch up.
At break, Marie found out more about her schoolmates, Carol and Beverley.
We'll have those, kid! Crisps stunt your growth!
Get off!
Leave the girl alone, you bullies! Have you no thought for other people?
Keep out of the way! You'll be sorry for this!
That's fine fightin' talk, but I'm bettin' that you're both cowards, deep down!
Later that day—
This'll teach that peasant not to tangle with *us!*
M. REAGAN.
Goodbye to her precious parrot! And I've got another idea that will get rid of her permanently! See you after school, Bev.
At four o'clock—
Poll! She's gone! But she couldn't have got out on her own! Carol and Beverley must have opened her cage!

*Marie went sadly home.*

How'd you like your new school, then, Marie? And where's Poll?

She got out of the cage. I've left it at the school in case she comes back. I've got a lot o' studyin' to do, Pa.

*Meanwhile, Carol and Beverley were putting the next part of their plan into action.*

Thieving brat! I know that blazer! I'll ring your school in the morning!

That's exactly what we want you to do!

Marie worked far into the night.
Multiplying numbers by themselves? So that's what they were on about! Squares and square-roots! Why do they use such fancy names for everything?
Next day, as Marie arrived at school—
The police here? I wonder what that can be about.
POLICE
Here she comes! She won't know what's hit her when they search her locker!

In school—
One of our girl pupils is suspected of stealing from a shop in the village yesterday. These officers are going to search the school unless the guilty person owns up.

search got under way.
We've searched the desks. We'll try the locker-rooms next.
As if any of *us* would steal anything!
In the locker-room—
I don't know why they're bothering with *our* lockers. We all know whose locker to look in—that peasant's! Her sort are always stealing!
Poll! You've come back! Good old girl!
when Marie's locker was searched—
This looks like the stuff that was stolen.
A JONES
L. EDV
But—but, I didn't put those sweets in there!
n, a shrill voice
led out—
the stuff in her locker, Carol!
the stuff in her locker, Carol!
Well, we seem to have a witness here! Which one of you is Carol?
Poll must have flown back into the cage and seen these two planting the stuff in my locker!

Carol and Beverley confessed to the crime.
All right,you two—down to the station. We'll have your parents brought there, too, so they'll know what you've been up to.
That's quite a bird you've got. It must have overheard those two girls, and it repeated what they were saying.
Later that day, things got back to normal.
All right, time's up, everyone. Hand your papers in.
MATHS TEST -1 HOUR
Well, that wasn't so bad. I'm glad I spent some time learning all that new stuff.
At the end of the day—
I've been looking at the test paper you did this morning, Marie. Considering that you've never done anything like it before, it was an excellent piece of work.
You were right—you really are a fast learner.
So I may be, but not as fast as Poll here!
THE EN

# Swans

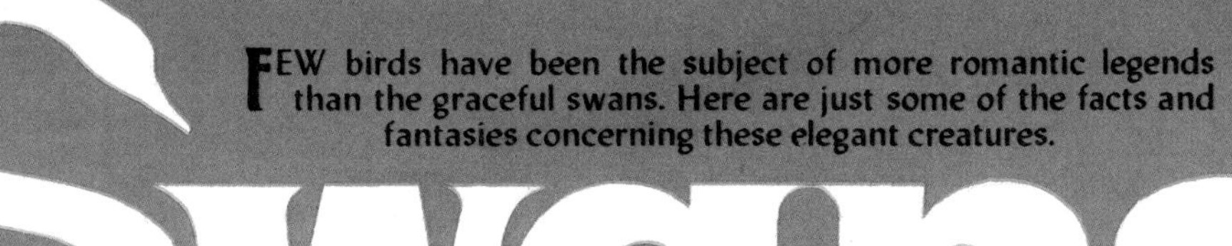

FEW birds have been the subject of more romantic legends than the graceful swans. Here are just some of the facts and fantasies concerning these elegant creatures.

In the famous ballet, " Swan Lake ", a handsome prince falls in love with Odette, a beautiful maiden who has been turned into a swan by a wicked magician. Only at night can she assume human form.

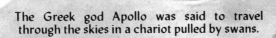

Until the introduction of turkeys from America in the 16th century, swans were the customary Christmas dinner—for the wealthy. When lesser fowl cost only pennies, a swan would fetch three shillings (15p).

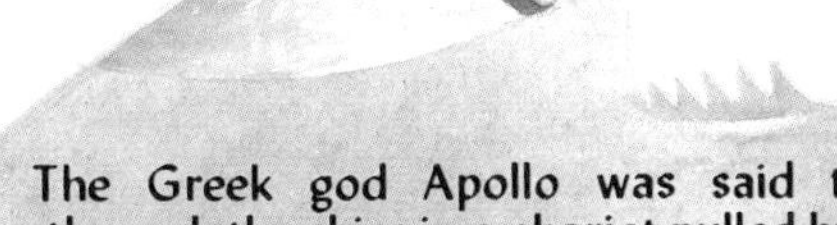

The Greek god Apollo was said to travel through the skies in a chariot pulled by swans.

Medieval legend told f the Swan Knight, ilver chain around his eck, who appeared in boat drawn by a wan. This is the origin f the swan wearing ollar and chain epicted on some old English inn signs.

# SWAN LAKE

WHOOPER SWANS

BEWICK'S SWANS WITH YOUNG

MUTE SWANS

Both parents help to build the nest, which can be floating,or semi-floating, and up to 4 metres across.

Swans' eggs are very rarely "egg"-shaped, but equally rounded at both ends. A Mute Swan's egg can measure 112.5 x 73.5 mm. One exception is the egg of the Black-Necked Swan, shown on the right.

Swans eat mainly aquatic vegetation, but also "graze" on shore. Mute Swans have been known to feed on frogs, tadpoles, worms—and even fish.

THE eight swan species are spread out through the world, as you will see from the map below; but our artist has shown all the different types together in this lake scene. In Britain, you are most likely to see the Mute Swan, but most of the other varieties can be viewed at bird sanctuaries or zoos.

This map shows the main concentrations of each species, world wide. Most swans migrate during the winter, though there is little movement between continents. Some varieties make overland journeys of up to 2000 miles.

# Pretty Papercraft

Next time you come across some corrugated paper in the house, try out these super ideas:—

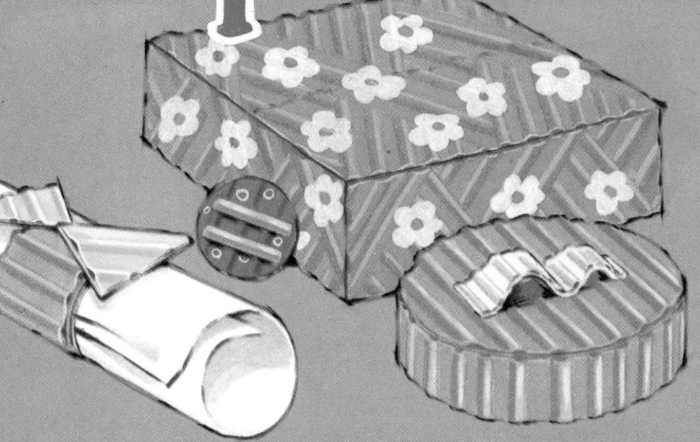

## NAPKIN RING

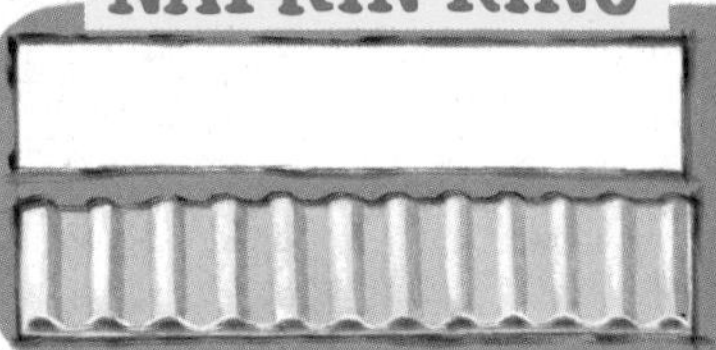

Cut a strip of stiff, white paper about 200 x 50 mm., then glue the ends together to make a ring. Repeat with corrugated paper, sticking it around and onto the paper ring. Cut two triangular pieces as shown and glue on top of ring. Decorate with poster or emulsion paint.

## BROOCH

Cut a circular piece of stiff,white paper and tape on a safety pin. Make a disc of corrugated paper the same size and glue onto the other side. Decorate as you like by painting or adding bits of corrugated paper.

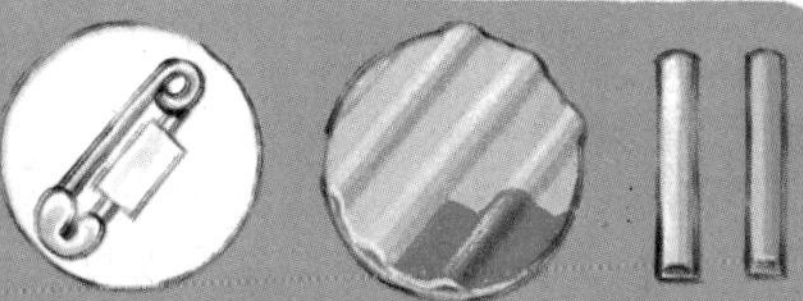

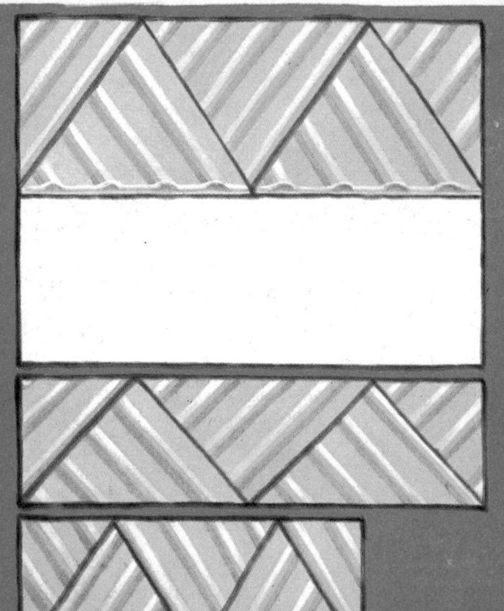

## TRINKET BOX

Cover a box with triangles of corrugated paper in the pattern shown here. The picture at the top of the page gives one example of how the finished box can be decorated.

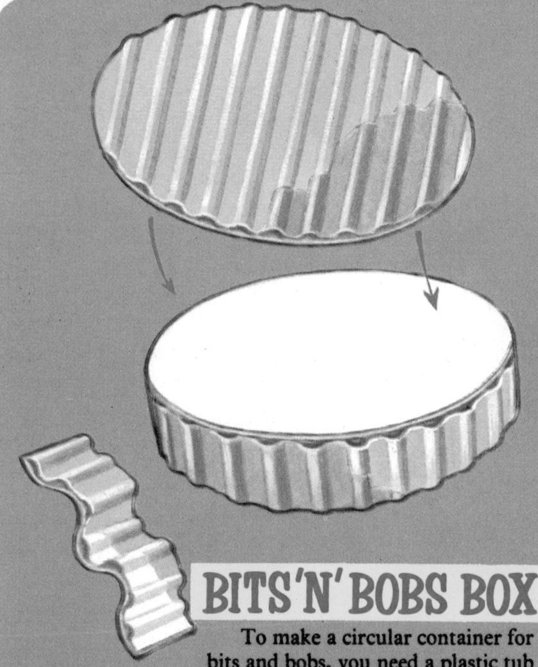

## BITS 'N' BOBS BOX

To make a circular container for bits and bobs, you need a plastic tub or cheese box. Cover the sides and lid with corrugated paper,then add an extra strip on top as a handle.

# The HERO

IT was Saturday, and Susan Carlton wasn't really enjoying an afternoon with her classmate John Meade. John was a Western fanatic.
Wyatt Earp wasn't really the hero that history made him. You see . . .
Oh? Fascinating!
I don't think!

Susan's sister, Rachael, wasn't enjoying her afternoon date with Alan Wright, either.
Watch how I release the rope a bit at a time. That way, even the steepest slopes are no problem. Great, isn't it?
What? Oh, yes, great!

hat night, in the girls' room—
Cowboys! That's all John can talk about! Never again!
And I never want to see another rock as long as I live! We'll have to dream up some excuses for next time they ask us out.

On Monday, at school—
Look out—here they come! Think of an excuse, quick!
Hey, everybody! Have you heard? Down by the river!

What about it?
There's a film company making a scene for a picture down there, and the star is Jason James!
Who's he?

Jason James? He's only the handsomest dream-boat you ever saw! We'll go down after school and see if we can get his autograph!
All this for some silly film-star? We'd better go with them!

So, that evening—
It's him!
Jason!
Hi, girls!
He looks perfectly ordinary to me!

We'd better take a break, Jason. We can't film with this lot here.
Sure, Harry. Say, we could get those press photographers to take some stills. Great publicity!

Why don't you two girls come into the boat? We can do a bit of still-work for the papers.
Ooooh! Jason, do you really mean it?

You guys shoot off all the film you want, while I take the boat out into midstream.
I hope he knows what he's doing. The current is tricky here.

But, when the boat reached midstream—
What's the matter, Jason? Why has the engine stopped?
No idea! I'm not an engineer, am I?

I push the button, but she won't start! We're drifting!
Couldn't you put down an anchor, or something?

Get some power on, Jason! You're heading for the weir!
Oh my gosh! Either of you girls know anything about boats?

Help! Help!
Hang on! We'll try to stop you!
This rope will come in handy!

John tied a slip-knot in the rope and—
Hey man, this is no time for rope tricks! Get me out of here!

Expertly, John lassoed a tree stump across the river—just in time!
The rope's stopped you. Hold on. Alan will help you ashore.

Here goes!
Alan! Be careful!

Me first! Get me off this thing! The kids can take their chance!
Get off me! Susan—can you go along the rope, hand-over-hand?
Anything to get away from him!

Don't try to go too fast. It isn't far to the bank.
I can make it, thanks, Alan!

All right, hero, you're next.
No! No! I can't! Look at that drop! I can't swim!

We'll have to slide him along the rope. Loop his ankles round the rope, Rachael!
Save me and I'll make it worth your while!

You push him, I'll pull.
Help! I can't look! I can't stand heights!
Oh, stop whimpering!

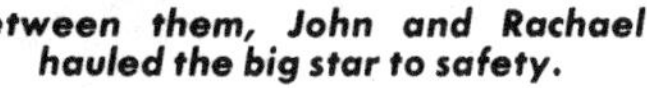
etween them, John and Rachael hauled the big star to safety.

You great dummy! 'ou've made a laughing-stock of this whole production!
Look—a stunt-man usually does those things for me!

But the crowd had forgotten Jason James.
Just a minute! John happens to be my boyfriend!
And Alan's mine!

Tell me some more about Wyatt Earp!
I'd love to go climbing this weekend, Alan!
I never thought we'd be grateful to Jason James!

**THE END**

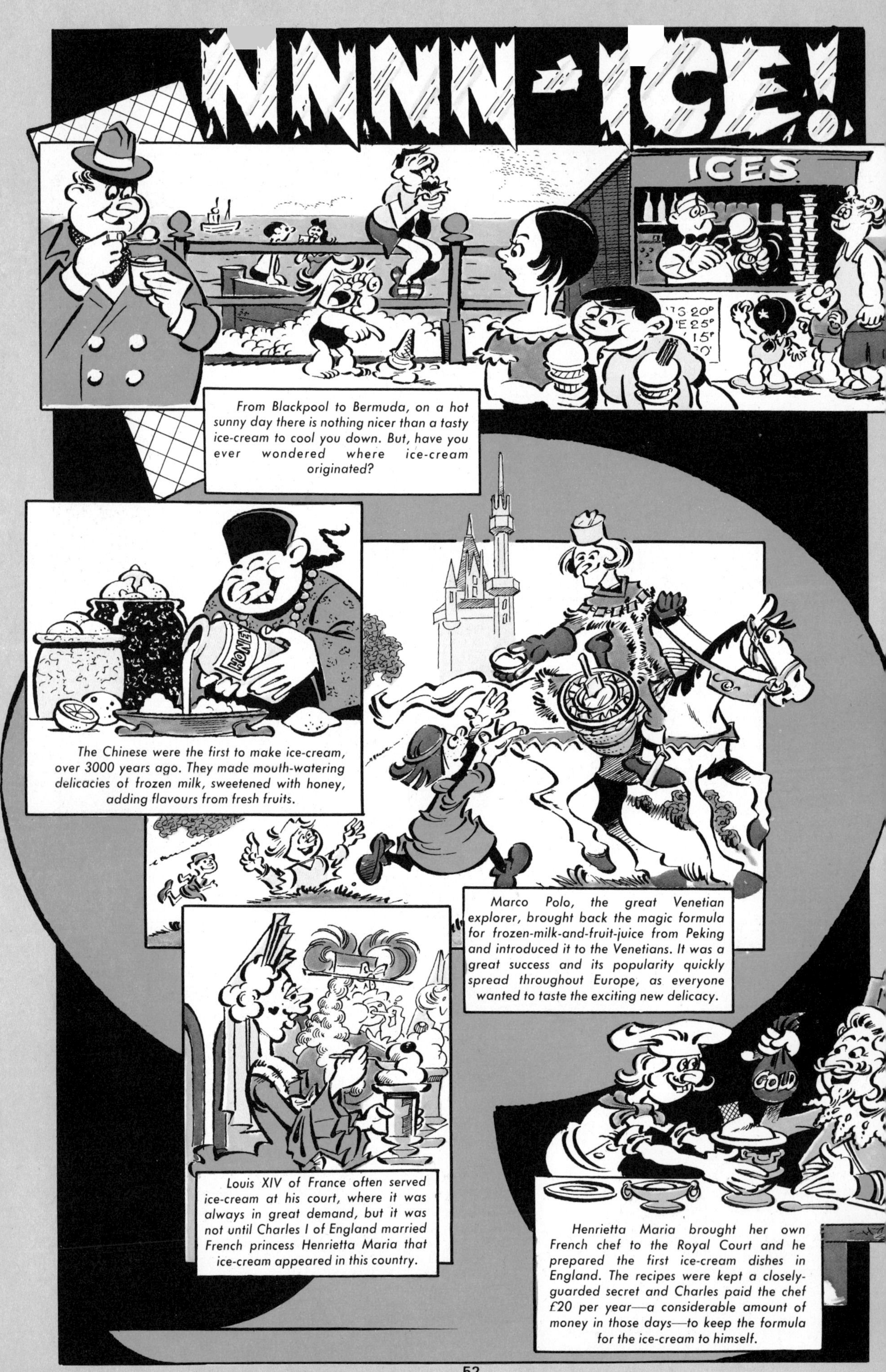

From Blackpool to Bermuda, on a hot sunny day there is nothing nicer than a tasty ice-cream to cool you down. But, have you ever wondered where ice-cream originated?

The Chinese were the first to make ice-cream, over 3000 years ago. They made mouth-watering delicacies of frozen milk, sweetened with honey, adding flavours from fresh fruits.

Marco Polo, the great Venetian explorer, brought back the magic formula for frozen-milk-and-fruit-juice from Peking and introduced it to the Venetians. It was a great success and its popularity quickly spread throughout Europe, as everyone wanted to taste the exciting new delicacy.

Louis XIV of France often served ice-cream at his court, where it was always in great demand, but it was not until Charles I of England married French princess Henrietta Maria that ice-cream appeared in this country.

Henrietta Maria brought her own French chef to the Royal Court and he prepared the first ice-cream dishes in England. The recipes were kept a closely-guarded secret and Charles paid the chef £20 per year—a considerable amount of money in those days—to keep the formula for the ice-cream to himself.

HOKEY POKEY
Not till the 19th century was ice-cream made available to the public. Italians who came to live in this country appeared on the streets of London selling the ice-cream from handcarts. The demand was so great that soon there were many vendors in other large towns throughout the country.
177
WALLS
STOP ME AND BUY ONE
ICE CREAM
In the early 1920's, a young man named Thomas Wall was the first to decide to sell hand-wrapped ice cream from his shop. Later, he came up with the bright idea of selling the ice-cream from a tricycle so that he could easily travel from street to street.
Other ice-cream manufacturers soon got in on the act. More and more tricycles appeared on the streets, then motor vehicles took over.
★ICE CREAM★
MRS ZIPPY
2
Not only was the method of transporting the ice-cream changing, so was the ice-cream itself. Manufacturers were producing lots of different coloured ice-creams in various shapes and sizes.
Now, you can buy your ice-cream in cones, tubs, assorted wrappers, wafers and even on sticks! It has certainly come a long way from the ice-cream the Chinese made all those years ago.

Dottie's Eating-Out Joke Book
I won't tell you again! Don't pinch the customers' chips on the way to the table!
I *told* you not to show off and try to speak their language when ordering in an Indian restaurant!
The gunga din
It's closing time!
CAFE
This soup is so cold, the fly in it is wearing a fur coat!
Whoever called this job ' waiting '?
Get a move on, chef! That bloke at table five is getting impatient!
MENU
I assure you it's not the same mince you sent back . . . *He's* eating that!
I'll try a karate chop, please,
ORIENTAL GARDEN

# CORA CUPID

CORA CARTER, who attended Palewell Comprehensive, considered herself a born matchmaker—but it looked as if she had a difficult problem with Milly Green.
I can't understand it, Phil. For a few weeks, Milly Green was the most popular girl around as far as boys were concerned. Now they run when they see her coming. What went wrong?
No idea, Cora. Hey, remember how she got to be so popular, though?
It had happened at the Palewell v St Cyprian football match.
What's happened? I can't see!
Jimmy Briggs has been knocked out by a flying ball!
'Phone for an ambulance, somebody!
Let me through! I know about first-aid!
Milly Green, whom no one had ever noticed before, took charge.
Give him some air! You . . . bring me a wet towel! I'll need something for a pillow . . . *and stand back!*
Hey! She really knows what she's doing, doesn't she?
Who *is* she?
After that, every boy had wanted to go out with Milly—and practically every one did.
That's the trouble, Phil — she went through boyfriends the way you go through biscuits! In six weeks, she'd dated every boy around who was available — and quite a number who weren't!
And there she sits now, alone and miserable — so what I want you to do, Phil . . .
No, no! I won't do it, whatever it is! I won't!
. . . is to spend an evening with her and find out what it is that turns off the boys.

So, that evening—
Milly, I just dropped by to hear your new LP. Remember, you said I could? Phil just happened to be with me, so I brought him, too.
But I don't remember — oh, well, you'd better come in.
I was practising my first-aid, but if you really want to hear the LP . . .
Oh, no! I forgot! I promised I'd do an errand for Mum! Look, you two go ahead. I'll be back as soon as I've finished.
She's so *obvious!*
Cora went to a café on the corner of the street, where she met some friends.
Phil's been with Milly for over half an hour. I'll give them the full hour. That'll be enough time for Phil to find out why she's the kiss of death.
Hey, Cora — isn't that Phil?
Well, it *looks* like him, but you can't really tell, can you?
Never realised he could run as fast as that!
Let me see, will you? Let me see!
Help! Keep her away from me!
Phil! What happened?
Get him a chair, someone! He looks really shaken! I bet I know why, too! Milly Green, wasn't it, Phil?
Cora, I've found out why Milly can't keep a boyfriend!
Is that what you wanted to know? It's because as soon as she gets one, she starts practising her first-aid on him!
Is *that* what it is? Why, the problem's not half so serious as I thought! All we need is some boy who's as interested in first-aid as she is.
Cora, you're wasting your time! Nobody around here's interested in first-aid any more–not after Milly's horrible example!
But there was someone, known so far only to Cora.
That boy who's come to live in our street. Goes to St Cyprian's, but otherwise he seems all right. Wants to be a doctor, so his mother told me.
And he didn't, as yet, know anything about Cora Cupid!
Hi, Harry!
My name's Joe.
Joe, then. Hey, your mum and my mum have become great friends, haven't they? Always drinking tea together and swapping recipes.

Look, what exactly is it you want? Can't you see I'm studying medicine . . . or trying to?
Going to be a doctor, aren't you? You must be dead intelligent. I suppose that's what attracts girls to you.
Attracts the girls? That's a laugh! All the girls I know don't want anything to do with a serious student. All they want is discos.
I suppose you're right. I've a girl friend in exactly the same position. She's studying a branch of medicine and just can't keep a boyfriend for that reason.
There's nothing she likes better than staying in at night studying her special subject, when the rest of us are living it up at the disco, but . . .
Hey, wait! Don't go away!
As a matter of fact, I'm just on my way to her house, to cheer her up. I suppose you wouldn't like to come along?
You suppose wrong! Lead me to her! To think there's a girl in this town who's actually interested in the same things I am!
Some time later—
So tell us again how you managed it, Cora!
Well, I just turned up at Milly's door with Joe and said we'd come to hear her new LP, then remembered I had to do an errand for Mum . . .
They've been there for two hours now. And I happen to know Milly's mum and dad are at bingo, so I think I'll just pop along and see how it's going.
We'll come with you, Cora.
Cora, do you reckon you should peep in through the window? It seems a bit off, somehow.
So it would be if it was just plain snooping. As it is, I'm checking on the progress of a very interesting case.
Two people with a common interest — each perfectly happy to help the other practise . . . practise . . .
Oh!
We'll — er — just leave them to it! They're sort of tied up at the moment! I'm not too sure if I've won this one, or not!
THE END

THIS CUTE WORKBASKET IS AN EXCLUSIVE DESIGN. IT'S MADE VERY SIMPLY FROM FOUR ORDINARY WOODEN COAT-HANGERS, AND YOU'RE GOING TO SURPRISE YOURSELF...
40 CMS
26 CMS
DON'T BE PUT OFF BY THINKING IT LOOKS TOO HARD! JUST STUDY ALL THE PICS CAREFULLY, THEN TAKE IT STEP-BY-STEP, STARTING BY GETTING FOUR COAT-HANGERS ROUGHLY THE SIZE SHOWN ABOVE, AND REMOVING THE HOOKS (SEE NOTE BELOW). DRILL* TWO HOLES IN EACH, AS SHOWN RIGHT.
ROD UNDER HERE
CORD
SHUT
DOWEL ROD
NEEDLEWORK
CARRY-ALL
SCREW
DOWEL ROD
WASHER
HANGER
YOU MAY GET DAD OR BIG BROTHER'S HELP FOR ONE OR TWO JOBS, MARKED WITH AN ASTERISK *
NOW YOU NEED THREE PIECES OF DOWEL ROD, AT LEAST 1 CM. IN DIAMETER, AND 26 CM. LONG EACH. YOU COULD ASK THE MAN AT THE D.I.Y. SHOP TO CUT THEM TO SIZE FOR YOU. YOU ALSO NEED SIX NO. 6 WOODSCREWS, ONE INCH LONG (SCREWS HAVEN'T GONE METRIC YET!) AND SIX WASHERS. SEE ABOVE HOW TO ASSEMBLE THESE, PUTTING TOGETHER THE WHOLE FRAME AS YOU SEE IN THE PICS. DON'T SCREW TOO TIGHTLY, OR THIS WILL STOP THE WHOLE THING FOLDING AND UNFOLDING. *OPEN YOUR FRAME AND TIE A STOUT CORD ACROSS EACH OPEN END, FROM DOWEL ROD TO DOWEL ROD, SO THAT THE FRAME OPENS TO 20 CM., AND NO FURTHER—I.E. TO HOLD THE BAG WITHOUT STRAINING IT.
THE MAKE-UP OF THE BAG IS SHOWN BELOW. USE BRIGHT MATERIAL, FIRST CUTTING A PIECE 54 X 26 CM., AS AT 'A', AND TWO END-PIECES, AS AT 'B', ROUNDING THE BOTTOM CORNERS, AS SHOWN. START ASSEMBLING, AS IN 'C', RIGHT SIDES TOGETHER, COMMENCING THE STITCHING 6 CM. FROM THE TOP, PUTTING BOTH ENDS IN SO THAT YOU HAVE A BAG (SEE 'D'). TURN THIS RIGHT SIDES OUT. FINALLY, FIX THE BAG TO THE FRAME BY HOLDING THE TOP EDGES OVER THE STRINGS AND RODS, AND GLUING DOWN FIRMLY.
PERFECT TO HOLD ALL YOUR EMBROIDERY AND KNITTING KNICK-KNACKS; EASY TO CARRY ABOUT; AND CAN BE FOLDED UP TO STOW AWAY IN A CORNER, OR A CUPBOARD.
MAKES A SUPER GIFT, TOO!
3 CM
26 CM
54 CM
A
6 CM
CUT TWO END PIECES 21 CM SQUARE
B
WHERE YOU FOLD TO
WHERE YOU STITCH TO
STITCHES
C
STITCHES
D
IT'S AN OPEN AND SHUT CASE!

# CIRCUS PONY

**IT was the sun shining on my face that woke me. I stretched luxuriously, then jumped out of bed. Pushing open the window, I leant out and took several deep breaths of the fresh country air.**

Fred, my big ginger cat, rubbed round my legs, purring; and Buster, our old dog who always sleeps on the end of my bed, came and thrust a cold nose into my hand.

It was going to be another lovely spring day and I couldn't wait to get outside.

"Come on, boys, we'll go down to the orchard before breakfast," I told Fred and Buster.

I scrambled into my old jeans and a T-shirt, ran barefoot through the house, crossed the lawn, and I was in amongst the fruit trees.

A soft whinny came from the far end, then the dull thud of hooves on the grass and Spangles, my pony, was beside me. He dropped his head and greeted Buster and Fred, then he rubbed his soft nose against me and blew gently. I put my arms round his neck and buried my face in his rough mane.

I say "my pony", but he isn't really. He's a circus pony and belongs to a small, private circus that the McHagarty family have run for as long back as they can remember.

The circus travels the country from April till October. The rest of the time, Spangles stays in our orchard and the old shed at the bottom, under the pear tree.

Any day now, Malcolm McHagarty, the grandson of the present owner, would be arriving to collect Spangles. The circus would be out on the road again and I wouldn't see them until the trees were bare and the winter weather was well on the way.

In one way, I looked forward to the spring, even though it meant losing Spangles. It was one of the few times I had a chance to see Malcolm.

"We'll make the most of the time we've got left, Spangles," I whispered in the pony's ear. "I'll go and have some breakfast, make some sandwiches and then we'll go for a really long ride together."

I always ride Spangles bareback, because that's the way he is used to being ridden, so it didn't take me long to get ready.

"'Bye, Mum—expect me when you see me," I called. "This might be the last time I can ride Spangles till October, so we're going to make the most of it. I've got some sandwiches and an apple for lunch."

"Have a good day, dear, but don't be too late," said Mum. "And don't go too far, will you?"

"OK, Mum," I called over my shoulder as Buster and I ran back to the orchard where Spangles was waiting.

**IT really was a glorious day. We trotted along with Buster lolloping behind.**

I sang as I rode down through the lanes and out across the moors.

By twelve o'clock, I was hungry and thirsty and I found a lovely spot under the shade of a hawthorn tree, with a busy little stream tinkling past. Buster had a good drink and so did Spangles.

They both shared my sandwiches and apple.

I stretched out flat on the grass with my hands under my head and enjoyed the feel of the sun on my face. I yawned.

" Hello, Polly. I've come to collect Spangles." The voice broke into my thoughts.

" Oh, Malcolm!" I said. " I knew you'd be here any day now, but I kept hoping for one more week."

" I would have waited a little longer, but Julie's had an accident and won't be able to do her act, so it's important to get a substitute rehearsing with Spangles as soon as possible," Malcolm explained.

" Poor Julie! Was it a bad accident?"

" Well, she broke her leg, so it's bad enough."

" Who's taking her place, then?"

" At the moment, it looks like me." Malcolm made a face. " I shan't be anything like as good as Julie, of course."

" Why couldn't I do it?" I suggested. " Spangles is used to me and I've practised Julie's routine on him lots of times, just for fun."

" That would be super!" exclaimed Malcolm. " You could live with my grandmother in her caravan, like Julie did."

It was wonderful, really wonderful, being with Spangles all the time; riding round in a bright tinselly dress like a ballerina, poised on one foot, then leaping gracefully through a hoop.

We travelled the countryside and Spangles and I were applauded rapturously everywhere. Gradually, we crept up the programme until we were " top of the bill ". We got better and better and more and more daring. I kept on bringing in new ideas.

One day a famous film director came to old Mrs McHagerty's van, said he wanted Spangles and me for a film, and he would pay me hundreds of pounds. The only trouble was, Spangles wasn't really mine and Julie's leg was better. I was due to go home any day.

I couldn't do those spectacular tricks on any other pony. Spangles was as much a part of the act as I was. Regretfully, I prepared for my very last performance. It must be good; it must be the best yet.

I gathered myself together and Spangles trotted round steady as a rock. I took a great leap and then—oh, horrors—I was falling, falling .....

**WITH a jerk, I came fully awake. I sat up rubbing my eyes . . . I'd been dreaming! How long had I been asleep?**

Buster had been asleep as well. He rose and stretched himself, just as I had done. Spangles was nowhere to be seen. Suppose he'd been stolen while I slept? Whatever would Malcolm say?

" Spangles! Where are you?" I called. I ran up to the side of the stream a little way, so anxious that I wasn't looking where I was going, caught my foot in a rabbit hole and sprawled full length.

A nasty, jagged sort

of pain ran through my ankle and I gasped with shock.

There was a soft snicker and Spangles appeared. He'd only been cropping the grass a little further up the stream.

Gosh, my ankle hurt! I tried tentatively to put a little weight on it, but it was too painful and already it was beginning to swell.

" What an idiot! What an idiot!" I muttered to myself. " Oh, whatever am I going to do? Mum'll be furious. She told me not to go too far or be too long."

The tears sprang to my eyes—part pain, part irritation—then Spangles really showed how intelligent he was. He put his head down and pawed the ground a couple of times, then dipped again—as he always does at the end of his performances.

Of course! Why hadn't I thought of that? If I grasped his mane and he lowered his back a little, I could get on without using my injured foot at all.

After several vain attempts, we managed it and I heaved a great sigh of relief.

" Home, Spangles!" I cried, slapping his broad back. " Come on, Buster—I reckon it's tea-time!"

We rode right up to the back door and, just as I was going to call Mum, she appeared—and behind her was Malcolm!

They soon had me off Spangles and sitting in front of the fire in the big farmhouse kitchen with my foot propped up on a stool.

How they laughed when I told them about my wonderful dream.

" It was lovely being a star and everyone clapping," I said. " When Spangles comes back in the autumn, I'll have to try some tricks with him."

" You'll do no such thing!" declared Mum. " You leave the stunt riding to Julie—she's been doing it since she first learnt to walk. It's in the blood, Polly, and you're a farmer's daughter, remember, not a circus owner's."

Then she bustled about and made the tea. There were hot buttered scones, with home-made strawberry jam—and, for a while, there was Malcolm. It was good to be home.

THE END.

# RAIN

THE rain had fallen constantly for eleven days and nights on the Canadian forest. The rivers had burst their banks and the lowlands were flooded, but still the rains came.
Marie Petain lived with her father, a doctor, in a log cabin in the forest. Their neighbours were a tribe of Red Indians.
Father! Anuak's come to visit us!
As Anuak came into the cabin, Marie gave him a towel to dry himself.
Anuak, my boy, have you reconsidered my offer?
I'd like to come to Vancouver and study medicine under you, Doctor Petain, but you know what the elders would say! They're very set in their ways.
Would you believe they're actually planning an appeasement ritual to the rain god, to stop the flooding?
Yes, I would. Old habits die hard.
During the night, Marie was awakened by a cry from the forest.
I could have sworn I heard something. Perhaps an animal is trapped.
Oh! There's someone there! Hello! Please come in out of the rain!
The stranger came slowly into the cabin and Marie brought food and drink.
Here you are. Let me take your blanket . . . No? Well, if you insist. You'll get pneumonia if you're not careful!
The stranger ate in silence.
Do you speak French? English? Algonquin? Atapasca?
Perhaps he can't speak at all.

At length the stranger finished his meal.
He's thanking me for the food.
You're welcome. Please sleep on the couch, if you wish. I'm going back to bed.
Next morning—
The rain's stopped at last! Thank goodness!
Oh, the stranger's gone—and just look at that water! He must have been drenched!
Marie began to hang damp rugs and blankets out to dry.
At least we'll be able to get this lot dry at last.
Oh! Hello, Anuak.
Good morning, Marie.
It's odd, isn't it? Last night the elders held the appeasement ritual, and this morning the rain has stopped.
Come off it, Anuak! Don't tell me you're starting to believe those old tales!
Marie's father came into the room.
Morning, Anuak. What's this, Marie? Have you been having a midnight feast?
Oh, that. No, it was just someone lost in the woods last night. I gave him some food.
He was tall, slim and looked like an Indian, but I couldn't say what tribe. He didn't understand any of the dialects I tried. Oh, and he wore a blanket in royal pattern.
He speaks no tongue known to man. No matter how much warmth there is,he is never dry.
Yes, that's right! Anuak! You're surely not suggesting . . .
It is *you* who saved the valley! Who do you think it was who came here last night? It was he . . . Rain himself! You gave him hospitality so he has gone away, taking the waters with him!
THE END

# OO-ER! LATE FOR SCHOOL!

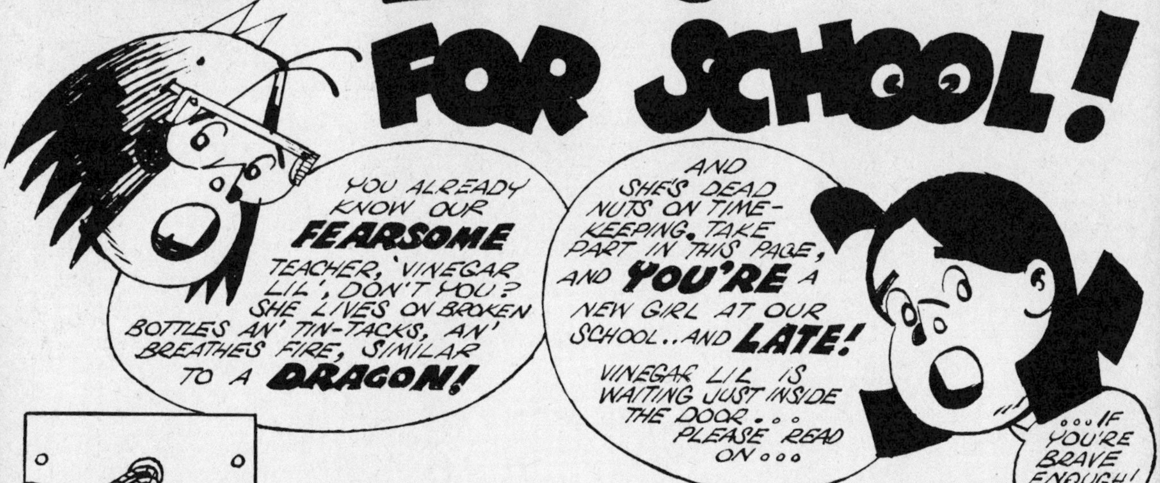

YOU ALREADY KNOW OUR **FEARSOME** TEACHER, 'VINEGAR LIL', DON'T YOU? SHE LIVES ON BROKEN BOTTLES AN' TIN-TACKS, AN' BREATHES FIRE, SIMILAR TO A **DRAGON!**

AND SHE'S DEAD NUTS ON TIME-KEEPING. TAKE PART IN THIS PAGE, AND **YOU'RE** A NEW GIRL AT OUR SCHOOL.. AND **LATE!**

VINEGAR LIL IS WAITING JUST INSIDE THE DOOR... PLEASE READ ON...

...IF YOU'RE BRAVE ENOUGH!

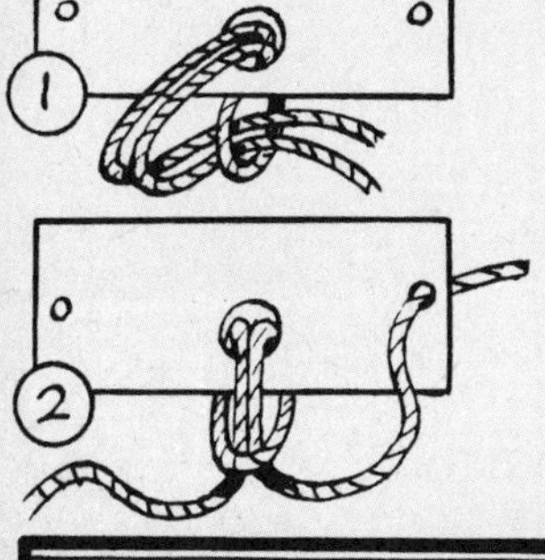

1

2

3

THAT'S VIN LIL BELOW, BETWEEN THE PICS OF YOU COMING TO SCHOOL AND THE CLASSROOM WITH YOUR DESK WAITING. PASTE THE WHOLE RECTANGLE ONTO STOUT CARD (OR TRACE OFF) AND CUT OUT. CUT OUT LIL'S MOUTH AND MAKE HOLES WHERE MARKED WITH AN ASTERISK. DO THE SAME WITH THE GIRL, AND YOU'RE ALL SET TO TRY TO GET INTO SCHOOL PAST YOU-KNOW-WHO!

FASTEN A 65 CM. LENGTH OF THIN STRING AS YOU SEE IN PICS 1, 2 AND 3. ALL YOU HAVE TO DO IS PASS THE FIGURE ALONG THE STRING FROM THE LEFT LOOP TO THE RIGHT. YOU MUSTN'T BEND THE CARD. IF YOU CAN'T DO IT, STAND ON YOUR HEAD IN THE CORNER, AND READ THE SOLUTION BELOW.

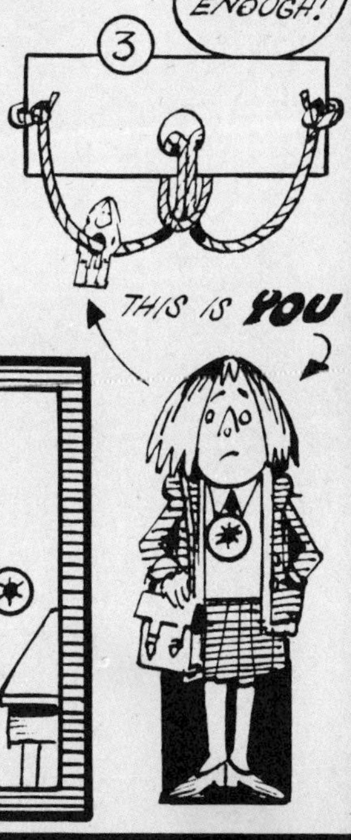

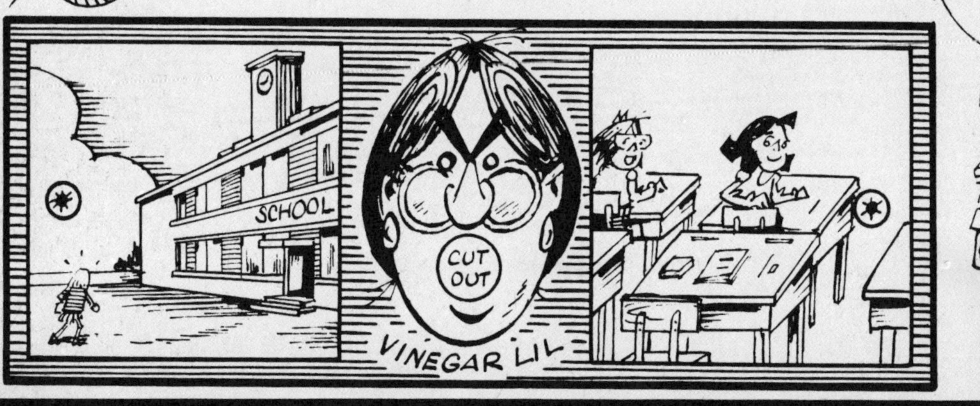

THIS IS **YOU**

SCHOOL

CUT OUT

VINEGAR LIL

## HERE'S THE SOLUTION - NO PEEKING!

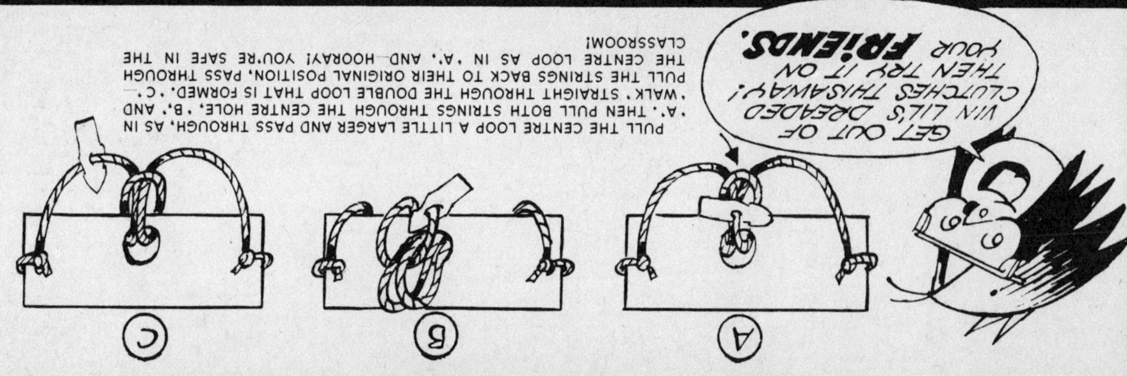

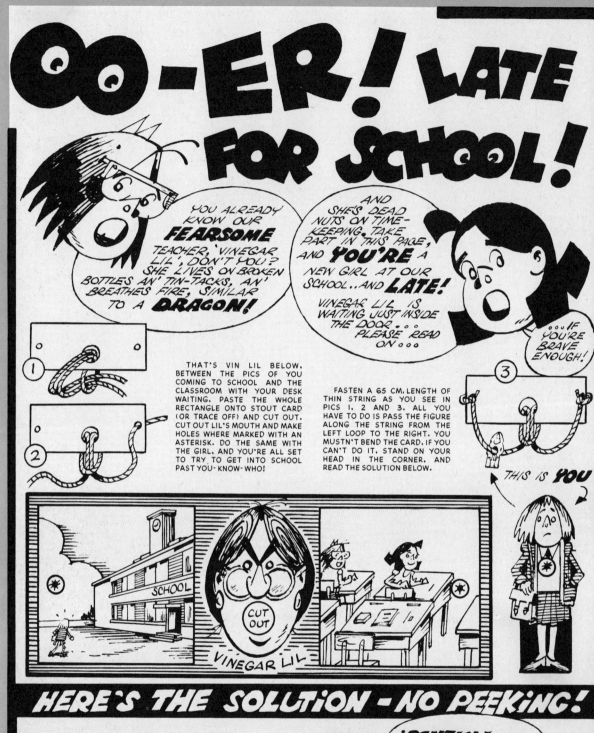

# JUNIOR NANNY

CHRIS JOHNSON and her friend, Anne, worked in a residential nursery for young children. One day, little Donny Smith arrived to stay while his mother was in hospital after a road accident.
Poor Donny looks so sad. We've tried everything, but nothing seems to cheer him up.
He's had a rough time, Anne. His father was killed two years ago and Matron reckons that's why he's so backward at talking.
n minutes later—
Rod and Les! Leave Donny alone!
You mustn't do that to poor Donny.
But Nurse Chris, he's a teddy-bear-leg-puller-offer!
He's a what?
Look what he did to my poor teddy!
And mine! Naughty Donny!
Oh, no!
Later, when the girls were preparing the children's tea, their boyfriends, Andrew and Colin, arrived from their nearby hostel.
Pulling legs off teddy-bears? You must be joking!
We're not, Andrew! It was horrible!
Then—
Boo-hoo! Donny did it!
Oh, no! This has got to stop!
ey hurried back to the playroom.
How would you like to have your own legs pulled off, young Donny?
Stop it, Andrew!
We mustn't tease him. The poor kid's had a tough life. The teddy bears' leg game is naughty and it's got to be stopped. But there must be a reason why Donny's doing it. It's up to us to find out.

Sorry Chris. I was a bit silly. I just wasn't thinking. I'll help you all I can.
Thanks, Andrew. I know you will.

Unny . . . unny! Want unny!
What are you trying to say, pet? Is it Mummy you want?

I'm sure it was honey he was saying—not Mummy. But honey's far too expensive nowadays for the nursery larder.
I've got some in my hostel room. It was a birthday present and I was keeping it for a treat. If that's what Donny wants—he'll have it. It will make up for my teasing him.

Ten minutes later—
See, Donny! Look what Andrew's brought you for a special treat! His birthday honey! Like some?

Take it 'way!
Oh, no!

Oh Andrew! Your precious honey! It's all my fault!
Nonsense, love! It was a hunch that didn't come off, that's all. Come on—we'd better clear up the mess before Matron turns up.

Later—
Read us a story, Nurse Anne.
Of course, dear. Which story tonight?

You know our favourite—the one about the bear."Isn't it funny that a bear likes honey. Buzz buzz buzz, I wonder why he does!"

Donny leapt out of bed and ran off.
All right,then . . . Hey, Donny! What's the matter?
Rod chose a sore subject there, but it's given me a clue about what may be the root of Donny's problem. When I've settled him back in bed, I'll have a word with Matron.

A little later—
I could be wrong, Matron, but . . .
It's worth a try, Nurse. Donny's mother's not well enough for hospital visitors, yet, but their next door neighbour has a key to the house. She may be able to help.

Early next evening—
Come and help me run the teddy bear protection league! I'm on my own while Chris has popped out on some mysterious mission.

Soon—
What's the idea, Chris? Been out on a dustbin search for old teddy bears?

UNNY!

What's it all about? Stop looking so smug, Chris and tell us what you've been up to!
It was Rod's poem that gave me the idea.

It struck me that Donny was missing more than just his Mum, and all the troubles seemed to involve teddy-bears and honey. So I put two and two together and did some investigations.

Matron entered the room.
As soon as Donny's mother regained consciousness, she wanted to make sure that he had his teddy-bear.
And the poor mite couldn't talk well enough to explain. So that's why he became a teddy-bear-leg-puller-offer!

Chris, you're a marvel! Fancy you guessing!
Well, with his own " unny " to cuddle, I doubt if Donny's going to bother about the girls' teddies any more—thank goodness!

And I've a honey to cuddle, too—eh, love? A very clever honey!
As long as you don't pull my legs off, I'm not complaining!
THE END

# Woollen Wonders

## Things to make with scraps of wool

## POM-POMS

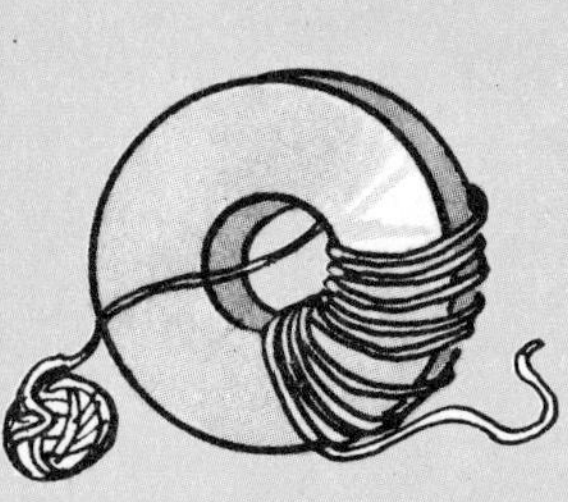

Cut two card circles with holes in the centre. Wind wool round until the centre hole is full.

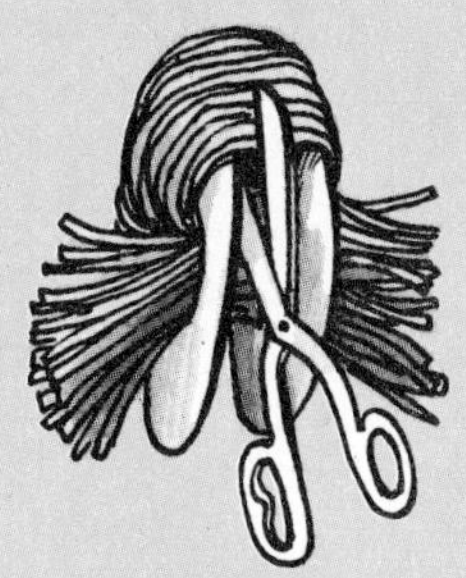

Cut the wool between the two cards, leaving the centre strands intact.

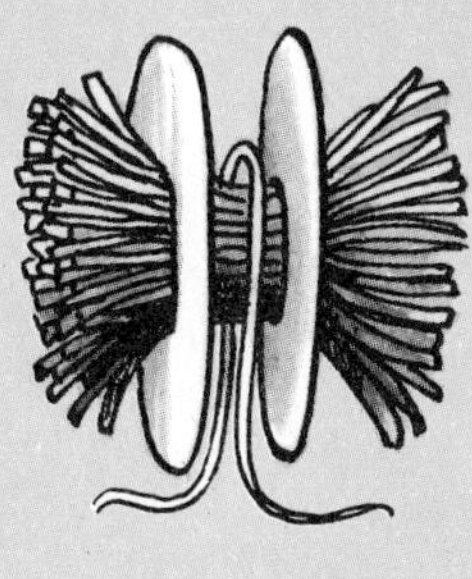

Tie a length of wool between the two cards to hold the strands in place then remove the cards.

You can join on a smaller pom-pom by tying these centre strings together. Add shapes of felt to turn them into animals or soft toys.

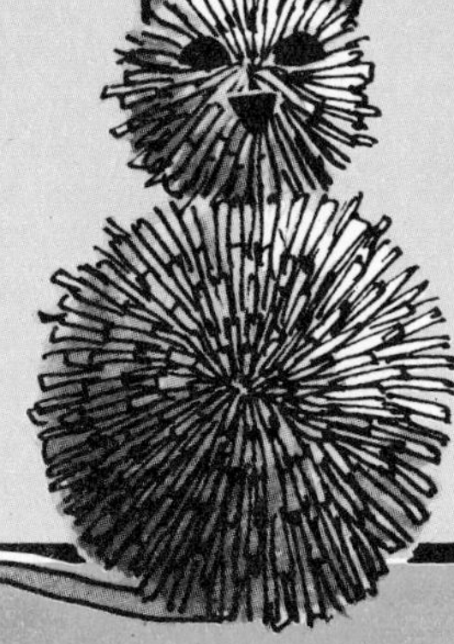

## GODS' EYES

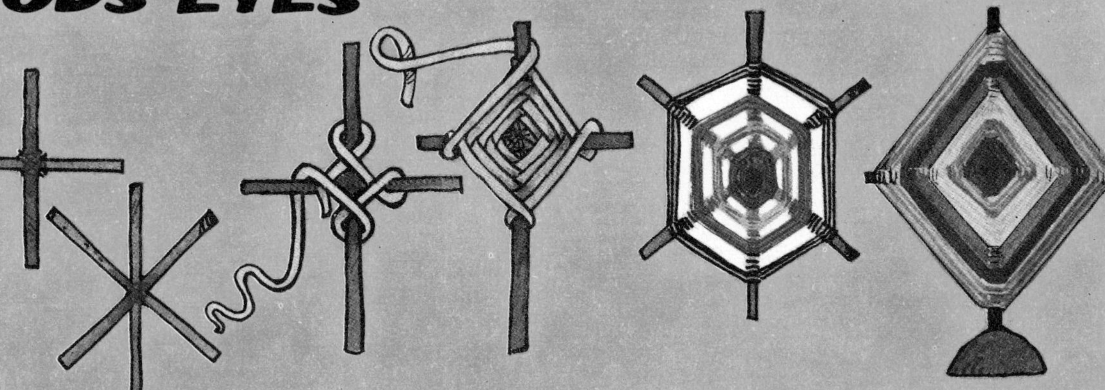

" Gods' Eyes " are Mexican designs woven round two or three sticks. The thin sticks are tied tightly together with strong cotton. Wrap some wool round the sticks in the form of a figure of eight. Add a new colour by tying the knot at the back.

You can make an in-and-out effect by reversing the pattern after a centimetre or two. You can also wind the wool two or three times round the stick at intervals to give a more open design. The finished piece can be made to stand with a base of modelling clay, or hung on cotton.

## CARD WEAVING

Cut a piece of stiff card 16 cm. by 10 cm. Measure 1 cm. spaces and cut V-shaped notches along the short sides. Wind a length of wool round the card and tie the two ends across the back. With about a metre of wool and a big needle, weave under and over, across and back, pushing each line tight. Vary the colours of the wool. Vary the weave by going over two and under two. Cut through the middle of the wool at the back when you have finished. Tie groups of two or three ends together to make a fringe and hold the weaving together.

Try a larger piece of card. Sew several woven lengths together to make a scarf, or sew the sides together and make a purse.

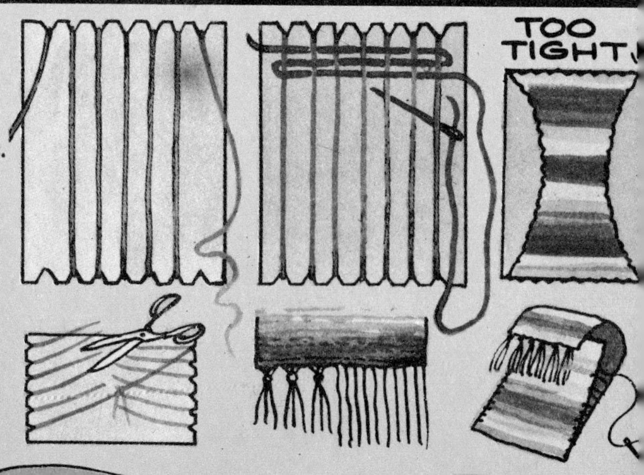

The Girl In The Looking Glass.
JANE MARTIN was spending a camping holiday with her parents in France. They were staying on a site close to an old chateau, but Jane was bored.
Does it say anything about the chateau in that guide book, Dad?
The chateau was built for the wealthy martin family, many of whom perished the Revolution. Other members of the ily escaped to England. Unfortunately, ne building is not open to the public."
Oh, what a pity. We might even be related to the family. The names are similar.
Mum and Dad don't care, anyway. All *they* want to do is lie in the sun. I wish I had something exciting to do.
There go the Dutch boys, off on their travels again. They've walked all over Europe and I'm stuck here. I can't even explore the chateau.
Still, I can always have a good look at it from the outside.

Jane pulled herself up and looked in to the grounds of the chateau.
It's beautiful! And so well kept—much better than I ever imagined.
I'll just tip-toe over the grass and peep through the window . . .
Please, mademoiselle, what are you doing here?
I-I didn't mean to trespass! I'm staying at the camp-site and I only wanted to look at the chateau. Are—are you the owner?
No, my father is—how do you say?—concierge . . . caretaker. The owners are away on holiday.
The boy's name was Jean. Jane then explained who she was.
. . . so you see, my surname is similar.
But that is most remarkable. I shall tell the Count of your interest when he returns in two weeks. You can meet him then.
I'm afraid we won't be here then. We have to go home next week.

I thought some of my
cestors might have lived
round here long ago. Oh,
ease let me look inside—
only for a few minutes.
The Count has a special reason for keeping out intruders, and the whole place is fitted with burglar alarms.

*Jean explained that, long ago, a curse had been put on the Lamartin family by an old peasant woman. If intruders ever tried to steal from the chateau and went unpunished, the whole place would be destroyed. If the thieves were stopped, the chateau would be safe for ever.*

I have to go inside and check one of the alarms. You can come in, too—but only for a few minutes. And you must promise not to tell anyone or touch anything.
I promise, Jean.

she stepped inside the chateau,
ane gasped with admiration.
Stay here, please. I shall return in one minute.

It's so beautiful—it's like something out of a dream!

Jane went into another room.
A room of gold and the portrait of a lovely lady in a gold dress!

The lady's name is similar to mine—and she even looks like me! I can't believe it!

LA COMTESSE JANINE DE LAMARTIN

What was that? Oh, it must be Jean. I'd bette go back. This place has strange atmosphere . .

As she turned to go, Jane saw the portra reflected in a looking glass—but it was her ow face in the picture.

My face in the portrait. I don't believe it . . .

In terror, Jane ran. She tripped over a footstool . . .

. . . fell to the floor, knocking herself out. At the same time, bells began to ring. Jane's fall had set off the automatic burglar alarm hidden under the carpet.

er, when Jane regained consciousness,
r parents and Jean were by her side.
Oh, I feel dizzy! Wh-what happened?
There were burglars in the chateau. They overpowered me when I went into one of the side rooms. Just as they were trying to force me to tell them how the alarm worked—it began to ring!
Jean's father arrived on the scene and the police were only minutes behind. They arrested the burglars,then you were found lying unconscious.
I remember! I saw *my* face in a portrait reflected in the mirror! I tripped and fell!
Oh, the trick looking glass in the Gold Drawing Room! Very old—and cleverly made. It distorts the real reflection so that anyone looking from a certain angle sees themselves in the portrait.
When they heard the news, the owners of the chateau cut their holiday short and returned a few days later. They held a special celebration for Jane.
I must thank you, Jane. But for you, the intruders would have got away with a great deal of valuable property, and the curse would have been fulfilled.
He's too polite to say I was an intruder, too!
And I have to thank the lady in gold. If it weren't for her, I wouldn't be invited to spend the rest of my " boring " holiday in a real French chateau! Oh! She's smiling! I thought that . . .
Smiling? No, no, look at the portrait itself.
Another trick of the mirror, my dear.
Is it? I wonder?
THE END

BERTHA had a large, cuddly dog called Big. Unfortunately, Big wasn't very popular with Bertha's dad.
Big 'n' Bertha
This old paddling pool of mine will come in handy in this heat wave, Big.
I hope you're not going to allow that hairy monster to play in the pool.
So, heed my warning! We'll tie this beast up, to be safe.
Later—
Seeing Big tied up has put me off playing in the pool.
. . . and then I flew into the water like . . . help!

you know what
happen . . .
" He'll splash Mum's washing . . .
Oh, dear!
. . . or even . . ."
Oh! What a mess! I'll have to do it all again!
decided to sunbathe
it's such a nice day.
Did I ever tell you about the time I won a medal for high diving? I was a great stylist, you know. Let me show you . . .
Big wants a better look— and no wonder!
Oh, no!
Dad's dire warning came true—but not quite in the way he thought it would!
THE END

# PONY CLINIC

GOOD MORNING!

I'M SARAH DANIELS, FROM LANCASHIRE. MY OTHER PONY'S EXPECTING A FOAL SHORTLY.

AN EXCITING TIME, SARAH.

THE BOOKS SAY A FOAL SHOULD BE HANDLED OFTEN, TO GET HIM USED TO HUMAN CONTACT, BUT MY FRIEND SAYS THE MOTHER ALWAYS RESENTS IT...

NOT ALWAYS, BUT QUITE OFTEN. DO IT WHEN YOU BRING THE FOAL IN, AT FIRST. IF THEY'RE BOTH AT GRASS, LATER, YOU'LL HAVE TO GET SOMEONE TO HOLD THE MARE WHILE YOU FONDLE THE FOAL.

AND REMEMBER - HANDLING DOESN'T MEAN **SPOILING!** I'LL COME OUT AND SEE YOU WHEN THE TIME COMES.

LATER

'RUBBER'

ARM

TEACH HIM QUITE EARLY ON TO WEAR A HEAD-COLLAR FOR SHORT PERIODS, BUT DON'T PULL HIM ABOUT BY IT. USE A STABLE RUBBER (CLOTH) TO RESTRAIN HIM, AND AN ARM AT THE BACK TO MOVE HIM FORWARD.

DON'T LEAVE THE HEAD-COLLAR ON WHEN HE'S OUT AT GRASS JUST YET.

THANKS, SAMANTHA. P'RAPS YOU'LL HELP ME WITH HIS TRAINING LATER ON?

# PET PROBLEMS

COME ON, PET-LOVERS!

I'M OFF TO MEET SARAH NAYLOR, WHO HAS TROUBLE WITH HER PET RABBIT, BORIS.

I'VE HAD HIM SEVERAL YEARS, DEBBIE. HE'S LIVELY ENOUGH, BUT SEEMS TO HAVE LOST HIS APPETITE LATELY

DO YOU THINK I SHOUL CHANGE HIS DIET OR SOMETHING?

IF YOU'VE FED HIM SUCCESSFULLY ALL THAT TIME, SARAH, YOU MUST BE ON THE RIGHT LINES.

NO, I THINK IT'S HIS TEETH. LOOK! THEY'RE OVERGROWN, AND IT SIMPLY MAKES IT INCREASINGLY DIFFICUL FOR HIM TO EAT.

A BIT LONG IN THE TOOTH, AS THE SAYING GOES. IT'S A PROBLEM THAT OFTEN AFFECTS CAGED ANIMALS. HIS TEETH NEED CLIPPING - A JOB FOR YOUR VET, NATCH.

APART FROM THAT, EYES BRIGHT, COAT GOOD - HE'S A CREDIT TO YOU, SARAH.

# A PAGE FOR A RAINY DAY

RECIPE FOR MODELLING CLAY
4 TABLESPOONS OF SALT
2 TABLESPOONS OF CORNFLOUR
4 TABLESPOONS OF WATER
4 DRIPS OF COOKING/OLIVE OIL
POSTER COLOUR.

COOK FOR A FEW MINUTES ON LOW HEAT, STIRRING UNTIL THE MIXTURE THICKENS. ALLOW TO COOL, THEN THE 'CLAY' IS READY TO USE.

SO IT'S ABSOLUTELY POURING OUTSIDE, YOU FEEL LIKE DOING A LITTLE MODELLING, BUT YOU HAVEN'T ANY CLAY. WHAT DO YOU **DO?** YOU MAKE YOUR **OWN!**

# WITCH IN A BOTTLE!

HAVE YOU HEARD OF THE OLD WOMAN WHO LIVED IN A VINEGAR-BOTTLE? THIS IS HER SISTER . . .

TO COPY OUR MODEL, ROLL OUT THE VARIOUS PARTS, AS YOU SEE IN THE PANEL AT THE LEFT. OUR MODEL IS 7 CM. HIGH, BUT YOURS CAN BE ANY SIZE TO FIT YOUR JAR OR BOTTLE.

PRESS THE PARTS TOGETHER, SMOOTHING OVER THE JOINS WITH A BLUNT KNIFE BLADE. MARK THE FEATURES, AND DRESS DECORATIONS, WITH A POINTED TOOL.

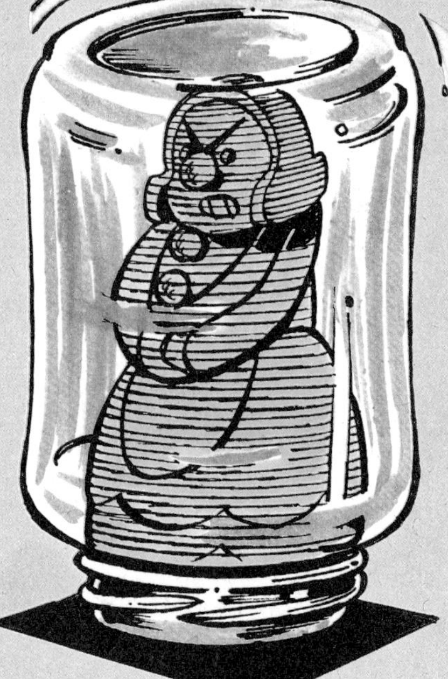

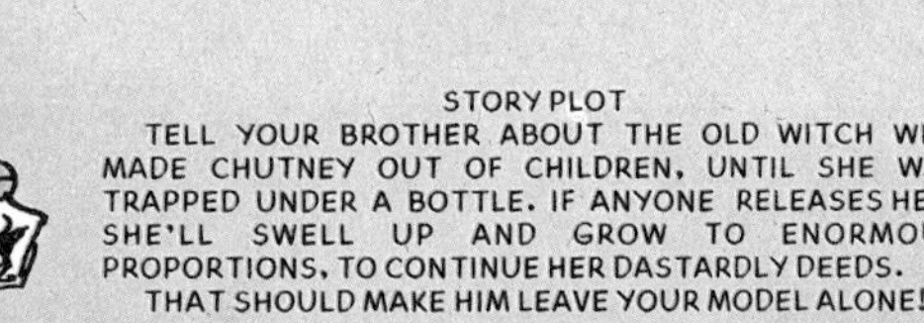

THE "CLAY" WILL KEEP FOR A LONG TIME, BUT TO PRESERVE IT, STORE IN CLING-FILM, OR A SCREW-TOP JAR. TO KEEP A MODEL FOR A LONG TIME, PAINT IT OVER WHEN DRY WITH CLEAR VARNISH.

STORY PLOT

TELL YOUR BROTHER ABOUT THE OLD WITCH WHO MADE CHUTNEY OUT OF CHILDREN, UNTIL SHE WAS TRAPPED UNDER A BOTTLE. IF ANYONE RELEASES HER, SHE'LL SWELL UP AND GROW TO ENORMOUS PROPORTIONS, TO CONTINUE HER DASTARDLY DEEDS.

THAT SHOULD MAKE HIM LEAVE YOUR MODEL ALONE!

**LOTS** TO DO! SOME "COOKING", MAKING MODELLING CLAY, A CUTE ORNAMENT TO KEEP – AND A SPOOKY TALE TO END UP WITH!

MAKE "CLAYS" OF DIFFERENT COLOURS, AND DESIGN YOUR OWN MODELS. PLEASANT TO HANDLE, AND HEAPS OF **FUN!**

# WEE SLAVEY

ON an afternoon off from her employment as a young maid in the Victorian household of Sir William Selby-Smythe, Nellie Perks wandered through the streets of London.
COOK'S COCOA
Coo, what a mean lot they are round here! You haven't collected much.
No, times seem to be bad.
Nellie decided to help.
Roll up! Roll up! You won't see better pictures anywhere!
Well, really! Fancy encouraging his daughter to stand in the street and beg for him like this! It's disgusting!
Lawks! It's Cook coming along the street!
Don't know what she'd have said if she'd caught me! Oh, lawks! Now it's started to rain!
Even the weather's against me,and nobody's interested in sitting for an unknown artist.
I'll sit for you. I'd love to have my portrait painted.
Nellie was delighted with the picture.
I'll sign it for you, Nellie. Who knows? If ever I become famous, it'll be worth money.
Much later, in the Selby-Smythes' drawing room—
Do hurry, Nellie. Our guests are cold.
As Nellie bent forward, the picture fell from her apron pocket.
What's this, young lady?
Oh, sir, it's nothing, really!

Where did you get this? Do you know the man who did the painting . . . this Ian Phelps?
Well, yes, sir.
My dear, it is Ian's signature!
I must go to him!
Lord Phelps began to explain.
Ian is our only son. We have not seen him for over ten years, since I paid his fare to Australia to start a new life in the colonies.
We must see him at once! Now that we know he is here, in London, we cannot lose him again!
Nellie offered to take them to the pavement artist.
I never realised you had such talent, my dear boy!
Your father has such plans for you, Ian. We shall help you to become famous.
A few weeks later—
You look very well, Nellie. Now, mind, don't go disgracing yourself with all those posh folk!
Fancy me, going to an art exhibition!
Nellie felt strange in the crowded gallery, until—
Nellie! Come along! I want to show you the prize exhibit!
Thank you for lending it to me, Nellie. It was the turning point of my life—that picture and the person who sat for it!
Coo! Fame at last!
THE END

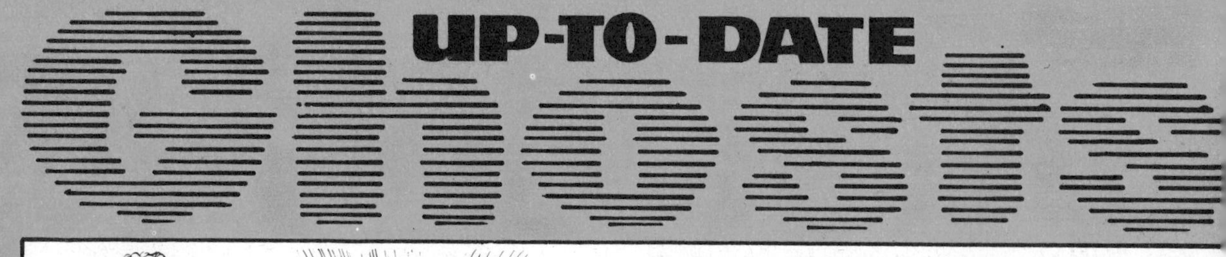

A ghost who likes modern appliances arrived at a house on the outskirts of Manchester when the lady who lived there bought herself a second-hand sewing machine. After she'd used it for about half an hour, the stitches changed size all by themselves; then, suddenly, the spools became tangled and the bobbin was flung across the room. This happened again and again until, finally, the lady said:

" Right! You can have it for an hour, then I want it back!"

This seemed to suit the ghost, because, an hour later, the lady was allowed to use the machine without any interference. She and the ghost shared the machine happily for years and then she sent it to a jumble sale. Presumably the ghost went, too—so if you're on the lookout for a second-hand sewing machine, you'd better be careful!

When an old hotel in Scunthorpe was being pulled down, the electricity was cut off weeks before, yet when the demolition squad moved in, they found the hotel's lift kept going up and down entirely on its own! The men were living in some rooms of the old hotel while they were working there and they were woken by strange noises and unearthly voices in the middle of the night. Then the lift began to work by itself. That was enough! The men moved out and found lodgings.

When it was time to wreck the lift, they cut through all the steel cables but the lift stayed put! The guide bars had to be prised off with crowbars before the lift finally crashed to the bottom of the shaft. Perhaps the ghostly passengers just didn't want the lift rides to end!

One Hallowe'en, the owner of a Derbyshire hotel unlocked the taproom door to find a man already standing there with his back to the fire. He had grey hair and he was wearing a neat, blue, pin-striped suit. But how had he got into the locked room? Just as the landlord began to question him, the man vanished.

The same hotel also has a more traditional ghost—a jilted bride who floats along the corridors in he wedding dress and on into the dining-room where th wedding feast was laid out but never eaten.

There are many stories of haunted stage-coaches galloping across the moors at night—but what about a bus speeding through the streets of London long after the scheduled services have stopped?

Not long before World War II, dozens of people reported seeing a Number 7 bus hurtling down an empty road in the Ladbroke Grove area of London. The lights inside the bus were on and there was no sign of crew or passengers.

After there had been a bad accident at a dangerous road junction on the ghost bus's route, it pulled up in a bus depot and vanished right in front of an astonished inspector. It was never seen again.

Where had it come from? Were did it go? No one knows. But if you're ever waiting for a bus at night and one appears that isn't on the timetable—don't get on it unless you're absolutely sure there's a driver in the cab. For, if you do—who can say where your journey might end?

Even more strange is the haunting of a giant electricity generating plant near Nottingham. What kind of ghost would you expect to find in a new power station? Well, if you saw him, you wouldn't even notice him, because he turns up for work dressed in blue overalls and a checked shirt. Mind you, he does seem to favour the night shift!

# APPLEBY FAIR

In June each year, hundreds of gypsies—or travellers, as they call themselves—set out from all over Britain and head towards Fair Hill, just outside the small market town of Appleby in Cumbria, to buy and sell horses.

It has long been a tradition to wash down the horses in the river in the centre of town before taking them to the selling area. It's a light-hearted chance for the travellers to display their splendid horsemanship.

The sales carry on all through the 'eek, although the main day is Vednesday. These three handsome orses were for sale singly, or as job lot. It is quite common for the ame horse to be sold three times in the ame day, each time at a profit.

When a deal has just been clinched, ll bargains are sealed the gypsy way y a slapping and clasping of hands. 'he agreed price, always in cash, is anded over immediately.

The picture on the left shows the simple, small wooden caravan of a young gypsy man whose only other possessions are the clothes he stands up in, and his pony. His dinner is a mixture of canned beans and ravioli. For some of the richer gypsies, like this Romany fortune-teller, home is a much grander affair. It is finished in stainless steel, has cut-glass windows, a fridge, cooker and colour TV. Instead of being horse-drawn, it is towed by a large, expensive car. But, in spite of having all the modern luxuries, the owner still has to carry her water in cans from a nearby tap.

# FOR ALL TO SEE

IT was Friday evening in Blackwood, and Lucy Weston was waiting for her mother to finish work. Mrs Weston was a widow, and times were hard.
Hi, Mum!
Hello, Lucy! Thank goodness it's Friday!
I meant to tell you—a letter came this morning from Canada. It was about your Uncle Charles—my brother. You never met him.
I've never even heard of him!
The rest of my family never approved of your father. They emigrated to Canada in 1949, and we lost touch. My sister-in-law, Grace—your aunt—has only written to me this once. Apparently Charles is very ill. He's also very rich—a multi-millionaire.
Gosh!
Lucy found out more about her distant family the following morning.
It's a letter to me from Uncle Charles. He says he's sorry for all the hurt he's caused, and wants to make amends. He says he wants to leave us something after he's gone, but his family would contest a legacy, so he's sending us something openly and for all to see.
And that's it—that document tied with ribbon? Let's see what it says.
CORN FLAKES
But, after they had both studied the document—
What does it all mean?
I don't know. It's full of " whereas's " and " heretofore's", so I can't really understand it.

Not long afterwards, Lucy's mother heard that her brother had died.
Do you suppose that this document from Uncle Charles is worth anything, Mum? Perhaps we'd better see a lawyer.
The following day they had a surprise visitor.
I suppose you must be my aunt and cousin. I'm Alan Weston, Charles' son.
Oh! I was sorry to hear about—
Never mind all that! When we came to sort out the old man's estate, fifty thousand dollars were missing. We know he wrote to you. Do you know anything about that money?
He sent us this a little while ago.
Let me see that! We've had to pay tax on the fifty thousand and we mean to get it! OK, so he left a million or so, but fifty thousand is fifty thousand!
This is all he sent? I might have guessed! This document is a title to some property in Canada!
Property in Canada?
CANADA
It's worthless! Look at the date—1959! In 1973, the government flooded that whole valley to make a reservoir!

The old boy must have been going soft in the head! He probably thought the land was still there! Here—the brat can use it for drawing paper! You won't be seeing me again!
Oh!

I'm sorry, Lucy. It was just a cruel joke.
But why should Uncle Charles go to all that trouble just to play a joke? Oh! Look at the time! I must be off!

Lucy did an evening paper round.
It doesn't add up. Nobody sends a letter three thousand miles just for a joke. I wonder . . .
A. JOHNSON NEWSAGENT
BOOKS
STATIONERY
CONFECTIONERY
GREETING CARDS
DAILY POST

Then, inside the shop, it came to her.
Hello, Lucy.
That's it! It must be! Hang on Mr Johnson! I'll be right back!
DAILY POST
STAMPS

What was all that about?
I don't know what's got into young Lucy! She dashed off as if her life depended on it!

little later—
Lucy! What is it?
The document! I think I know what it's all about! It's in this drawer, isn't it?
Lucy was breathless by the time she returned to the shop.
You know all about these things! What d'you make of that?
It's just an old document. I . . . wait a minute!
ucy knew that the newsagent was a keen stamp collector.
Lucy! Is this yours? It's a 1959 St Lawrence Seaway printing error! It must be worth over twenty thousand pounds!
STAMPS
PAPERBACKS
Yes—almost fifty thousand dollars!
Take that home and put it in a safe place!
" Openly and for all to see", the old man said! It was so obvious, none of us could see it! It really was a joke—but it wasn't a joke on us!
THE END

# HOTHAM PARK ZOOTOPIA

miniature railway and boating pool

HELLO! I'M CLARE! IF YOU LIKE ANIMALS, JOIN ME ON MY DAY OUT.
FIRST, MEET SUZY THE PONY AND HER KEEPER, MARTIN BURCH.

IT'S ONE THING BEING OFFERED A KISS BY A GOAT . . .


"... but quite another to get a hug from a bear."

"I didn't even offer the poor pig a pat!"

d rather fuss over a lop-eared rabbit."

" The fox looked foxy . . ."

. so I went to chat with a chimp."

" I paid a quick visit to this super fairy-tale castle."

THE HEAD KEEPER, GORDON BROWN, LET ME HOLD THIS SILKY BANTAM CHICK.
JUST TIME FOR ONE WISH BEFORE I GO HOME. I KNOW, I'LL WISH I CAN COME BACK HERE TOMORROW INSTEAD OF GOING TO SCHOOL!

**If you would like to visit the zoo, the address is: Zootopia, Hotham Park, Bognor Regis, Sussex.**

# THE HELPERS

FAR out on the edge of our galaxy, the robot ship, Philos 9, approached a planet. On board the craft were Officers Petra Sardos and Anya Malenka. Their mission was to help the primitive races on young planets.

Uncharted planet dead ahead. Recommend exploration.

Preliminary reports suggest planet habitable.

Let's go down and have a look, Anya.

Gravity, one point one; atmosphere,oxygen based. Dominant life-form appears to be bipedal hominid. Starting landing routine.

It's just like home!
They said at the academy that this sort of planet tends to produce people rather like us.
This should be a good hiding place for the ship.
It must have been like this back home at one time.
A scan of the area by photopilot gave Petra and Anya an idea of what to expect.
Yes, they're humans, all right. Early stone age, I'd say. No evidence of fire, wheel, or smelting.
They wear skins, so we'd better get some, too.
Next morning, Officers Sardos and Malenka set off towards the nearby settlement.
Ugh! These skins itch!
You'll have to get used to it. You'll be wearing them for the next six months.

The settlement was primitive, but not unfriendly.
Sumac anuit sinasu aranak?
Well, at least they're not trying to spear us! What do you suppose he means?
You're supposed to be the linguist . . . you figure it out!
Petra and Anya had been well trained, and, over the next weeks, they put their knowledge to good use.
Asanu! Asanu!
That's right . . . like the sun, only smaller. It is called fire.
Later—
I'm getting some good recordings of the language. The computer should be able to sort the bits that puzzle us.
Good . . . then you can come and help me. It's cookery this afternoon.
The cave-dwellers learned fast, and, with the help of the computer, Petra and Anya soon came to understand their primitive language.
Yes, that's it. Make two of these wheels and you can build a cart.
Burn the special stone and the metal will flow out. Catch it in the shape you need . . . see?
Magic!

Not magic, Ornac . . . technology!
This teknajee is good!
All too soon, it was time for the space officers to leave.
Our work is done, Ornac, so we must leave.
Leave? Stay, and be with us always, mighty dwaghes!
Dwaghes? That means gods in their language!
If they're starting to believe that, it's time we left, before they become dependent on us.
They made their farewells and left hurriedly that night.
Pity, I was beginning to like this planet.
There are plenty more.

And, on the ground—
See the fire in the sky? The dwaghes shall be with us always—in spirit.
And, in their honour, we shall call our land after their strange names. Henceforth it will be known as Petranya.
Centuries later, the descendants of Ornac's people again met strange visitors. These people from afar had not come to teach, but to conquer.

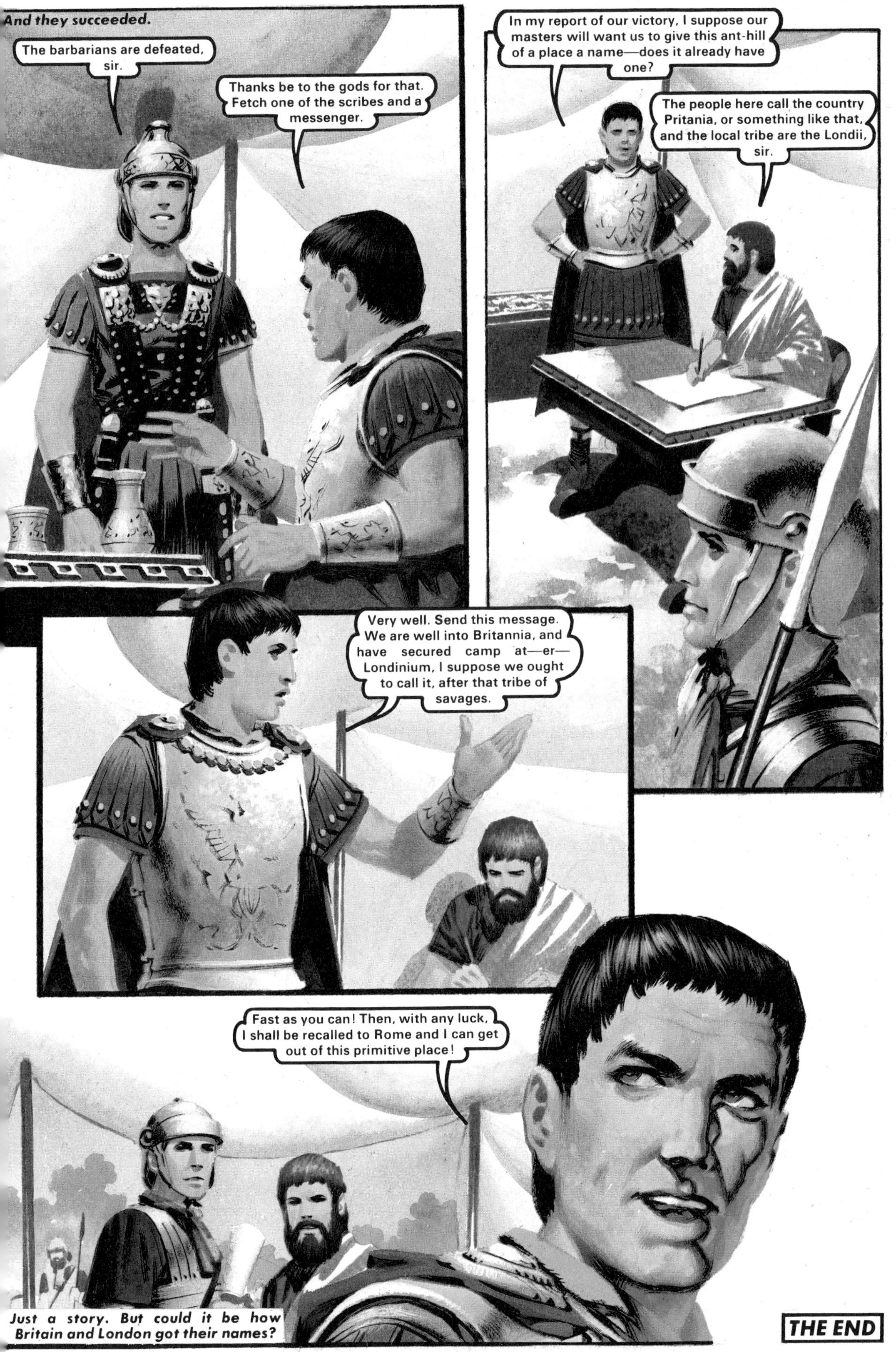
And they succeeded.
The barbarians are defeated, sir.
Thanks be to the gods for that. Fetch one of the scribes and a messenger.
In my report of our victory, I suppose our masters will want us to give this ant-hill of a place a name—does it already have one?
The people here call the country Pritania, or something like that, and the local tribe are the Londii, sir.
Very well. Send this message. We are well into Britannia, and have secured camp at—er—Londinium, I suppose we ought to call it, after that tribe of savages.
Fast as you can! Then, with any luck, I shall be recalled to Rome and I can get out of this primitive place!
Just a story. But could it be how Britain and London got their names?
THE END

# HOUSE OF BEAUTY

The National Butterfly Museum is in this beautiful old house near Bramber Castle, West Sussex. St Mary's, built in the 12th century, was enlarged and redesigned 300 years later and it was in this house that Queen Elizabeth I stayed when she visited Bramber in 1585.

Charles II hid in St Mary's after being defeated at the Battle of Worcester. This is the room—complete with secret panel—where he spent his last night in England before going into exile.

Nowadays, it's not kings and queens bu ordinary people who come to look at the house, its beautiful rooms and its collections. Here is part of a collection of coral, shells and birds.

By far the largest and most important collection in the house is that in The National Butterfly Museum. There are about a million butterflies and moths from all over the world at St Mary's.

A Giant Atlas Moth is a collector's item, but people also buy this to frame and hang like a picture.

In the shop at St Mary's, among other souvenirs, you can find dozens of butterflies and moths of all colours and sizes and at a wide range of prices, some surprisingly cheap. If you are interested in butterflies, you could become an observer or even a breeder—but please don't catch and kill wild butterflies. There are not enough about.

DESK CALENDAR 1984

| JANUARY | |
|---|---|
| Su. | 1 8 15 22 29 |
| M. | 2 9 16 23 30 |
| Tu. | 3 10 17 24 31 |
| W. | 4 11 18 25 |
| Th. | 5 12 19 26 |
| F. | 6 13 20 27 |
| S. | 7 14 21 28 |

| FEBRUARY | |
|---|---|
| Su. | 5 12 19 26 |
| M. | 6 13 20 27 |
| Tu. | 7 14 21 28 |
| W. | 1 8 15 22 29 |
| Th. | 2 9 16 23 |
| F. | 3 10 17 24 |
| S. | 4 11 18 25 |

| MARCH | |
|---|---|
| Su. | 4 11 18 25 |
| M. | 5 12 19 26 |
| Tu. | 6 13 20 27 |
| W. | 7 14 21 28 |
| Th. | 1 8 15 22 29 |
| F. | 2 9 16 23 30 |
| S. | 3 10 17 24 31 |

| APRIL | |
|---|---|
| Su. | 1 8 15 22 29 |
| M. | 2 9 16 23 30 |
| Tu. | 3 10 17 24 |
| W. | 4 11 18 25 |
| Th. | 5 12 19 26 |
| F. | 6 13 20 27 |
| S. | 7 14 21 28 |

| MAY | |
|---|---|
| Su. | 6 13 20 27 |
| M. | 7 14 21 28 |
| Tu. | 1 8 15 22 29 |
| W. | 2 9 16 23 30 |
| Th. | 3 10 17 24 31 |
| F. | 4 11 18 25 |
| S. | 5 12 19 26 |

| JUNE | |
|---|---|
| Su. | 3 10 17 24 |
| M. | 4 11 18 25 |
| Tu. | 5 12 19 26 |
| W. | 6 13 20 27 |
| Th. | 7 14 21 28 |
| F. | 1 8 15 22 29 |
| S. | 2 9 16 23 30 |

| JULY | |
|---|---|
| Su. | 1 8 15 22 29 |
| M. | 2 9 16 23 30 |
| Tu. | 3 10 17 24 31 |
| W. | 4 11 18 25 |
| Th. | 5 12 19 26 |
| F. | 6 13 20 27 |
| S. | 7 14 21 28 |

Fill in this space by sticking on a photograph of your favourite pet.

| AUGUST | |
|---|---|
| Su. | 5 12 19 26 |
| M. | 6 13 20 27 |
| Tu. | 7 14 21 28 |
| W. | 1 8 15 22 29 |
| Th. | 2 9 16 23 30 |
| F. | 3 10 17 24 31 |
| S. | 4 11 18 25 |

| SEPTEMBER | |
|---|---|
| Su. | 2 9 16 23 30 |
| M. | 3 10 17 24 |
| Tu. | 4 11 18 25 |
| W. | 5 12 19 26 |
| Th. | 6 13 20 27 |
| F. | 7 14 21 28 |
| S. | 1 8 15 22 29 |

| OCTOBER | |
|---|---|
| Su. | 7 14 21 28 |
| M. | 1 8 15 22 29 |
| Tu. | 2 9 16 23 30 |
| W. | 3 10 17 24 31 |
| Th. | 4 11 18 25 |
| F. | 5 12 19 26 |
| S. | 6 13 20 27 |

| NOVEMBER | |
|---|---|
| Su. | 4 11 18 25 |
| M. | 5 12 19 26 |
| Tu. | 6 13 20 27 |
| W. | 7 14 21 28 |
| Th. | 1 8 15 22 29 |
| F. | 2 9 16 23 30 |
| S. | 3 10 17 24 |

| DECEMBER | |
|---|---|
| Su. | 2 9 16 23 30 |
| M. | 3 10 17 24 31 |
| Tu. | 4 11 18 25 |
| W. | 5 12 19 26 |
| Th. | 6 13 20 27 |
| F. | 7 14 21 28 |
| S. | 1 8 15 22 29 |

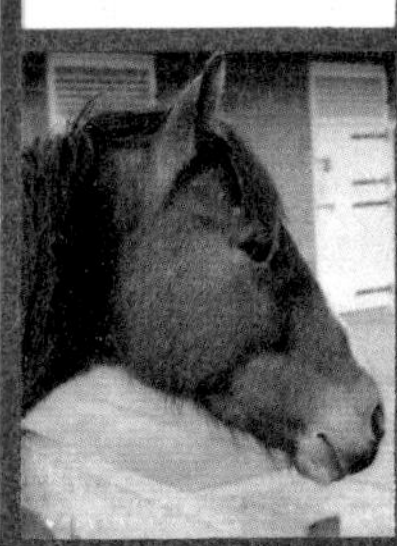

***Instructions overleaf—***

# Simple to make

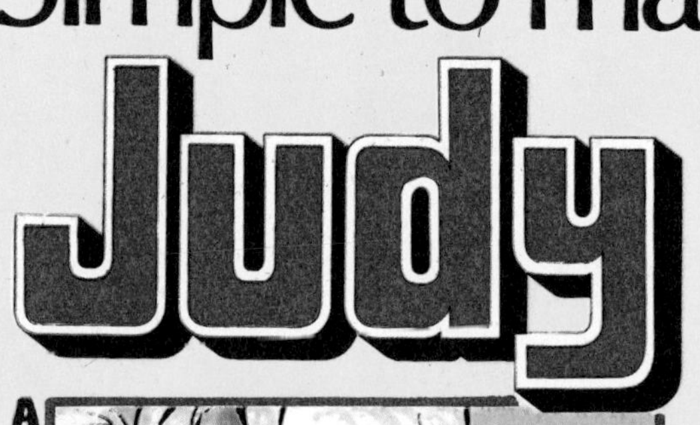


# DESK CALENDAR

Cut around the thick outside red line. Fold along the black dotted lines.

Glue blue area and join up with the underside of A, as shown above.

# THE THEATRE

TRAVELLING home after a visit to a sick relative, Grace Simpson found herself stuck in the town of Redington. With a few hours to spare before her train connection, she went for a walk.
A theatre! That's more like it! Just the place for me to get in out of the rain and cheer myself up a bit.

As there was no-one at the pay desk, Grace walked right in.
It's late, so I've probably missed a good bit of the show, but these acrobats certainly look worth watching.
I'm beginning to feel that Redington isn't such a bad place after all!
HURRAH
CHEER
Then the lights came up.
But . . . they're all dressed in the fashion of a hundred years ago! How can that be? Unless . . .
Silence, Ladies and Gentlemen, *please!* Encouraged as I am by your enthusiastic reception for that avalanche of acrobatic agility . . .
. . . unless they're all ghosts! One thing's for sure, I'm not staying here to find out!
There was another explanation, b
Grace was too taken by surprise
think of it.

EXIT
Hey, you there—
come back!
Oh, no—they're coming after
me!
Then—
Aaaaah!
Sorry, miss, but we couldn't
just let you run off like that!
THEATRE
It's no wonder you got a fright,
seeing us dressed like this. But there's
quite a simple explanation, really.
Eh?
You see, you've come in in the
middle of "The Grand Old Days"
—where the audience dress up
in Victorian clothes just for the
fun of it!
Of course! I should have
guessed!

Grace's new-found friends insisted she stay on and see the show as their guest.
And now, Miss Mollie Mallon—to provide you with a terpsichorean treat that will titillate the tiredest taste!
O-O-O-O-O-OH!
That M.C.'s absolutely brilliant!
Michael Manners? Yes, he is quite unique.
Grace could not remember when she had enjoyed herself more, but then—
Come on, miss, time you left. You don't want to miss that train, do you?
SECOND INTERVAL
You wouldn't like it much after the second interval, anyway. We only stay because, as members, we have to.
But my train doesn't go for another half hour!
But they did not listen and Grace was politely, but firmly, ushered out.
I suppose they were right. This way, I'll be able to take my time walking to the station.
But, 10 minutes later—
Oh! I've left my gloves back in the theatre! And I'll have to run if I'm to get them back and still catch that train!

Now then, miss, is everything all right?
It's quite all right, officer. You see, I left my gloves in the Imperial and I'm rushing back to get them before my train goes.
Well, I've heard some unlikely stories in my time—but that's the best yet!
But it's the truth, every word of it!
No, it isn't—because the Imperial was burnt to the ground exactly a year ago tonight. It happened during a performance of " The Grand Old Days "—just after the second interval, as Michael Manners was introducing the next act. None of the audience survived.
IMPERIAL THEATRE
THE GRAND OLD DAYS
And perhaps you're wondering if Grace Simpson ever found her gloves again? Well she did, actually, only they weren't much use to her any more. You see—they were so charred as to be almost unrecognisable.
THE END

# A BRUSH

**I TIPTOED round the corner of the house, because I guessed that Ben would be asleep. The afternoon was hot and sultry; just the sort of day to be out on our tiny patch of grass by the lilac bushes, gently snoozing through the midday heat.**

Yes, there he was, just as I'd thought, stretched out on the garden swing chair, looking as if he hadn't a care in the world.

"It's a shame to wake him," I muttered as I pulled Dad's newspaper carefully out from under Ben's head and sat down on the tartan rug in front of him.

Anyway, there was no hurry, as Mum was busy making P.C. Watson a cup of tea. It was a good thing that P.C. Watson was a friend of Dad's, for maybe this business would be sorted out without any trouble.

When Mum had opened the door to a policeman and had heard why he had come, she had been horrified and indignant at the same time, like me. But, whereas I didn't really believe P.C. Watson, she did.

"Go and get Ben at once, Cassie," she had said, looking red and embarrassed. "P.C. Watson must see him."

I sighed now and stretched my legs. Ben's black, curly hair was rumpled and he looked so innocent, but, of course, Mum had said all along that we didn't know

anything about Ben's past.

I supposed he could have been in trouble before, for all we knew. But he had been a good friend to me—more than a friend, really—and I just didn't know what I'd do without his company now.

"I do wish Ben was a bit neater and tidier, Cassie," Mum had complained several times at the beginning.

"Oh, Mum!" I'd said. "Don't be so old-fashioned! You shouldn't judge by appearances. You're always saying so yourself."

Mum had to admit, later on, that she had been very wrong about Ben.

"You couldn't find a kindlier, more friendly character," she'd said; and we'd all agreed—even Dad.

**THAT was why P.C. Watson's accusation seemed so crazy. He hadn't actually used the word menacing, but you could tell it was there, hovering at the back of his mind.**

It was a nasty word at the best of times, and in connection with Ben, it was plain ridiculous.

"Supposing they take Ben away?" I whispered. "What shall I do?"

I felt my eyes prick with tears as I gazed sadly at Ben, then I shook myself. I must snap out of it. What I needed was something like a session on the trampoline down

# WITH THE LAW

at the club to jolt me out of such melodramatic ideas.

Odd, thinking of that, though, because I had been coming back from the club one spring evening when I'd first seen Ben. He had been swinging along on the opposite pavement and he had given me a sort of sidelong glance. I hadn't taken much notice.

Next day, I'd seen him in practically the same spot. The day after, he had come boldly up to me, obviously counting three meetings in a row as an excuse for getting acquainted. In the end I'd taken him home for a meal.

"I don't know what your dad will say, Cassie," Mum had said, when I'd gone in first to warn her of a visitor.

But I had known that I could deal with Dad. After all, daughters have to grow up and discover their own friends.

"Cassie! Ben! Where are you?" Mum's shout broke into my thoughts. "Come on! Constable Watson hasn't got all day!"

Hurriedly I scrambled up. Would it be an idea, I wondered, to persuade Ben to go out the back gate and then I could tell Mum he'd disappeared?

No, I thought; better not. That wouldn't solve anything. They'd only catch up with him in the end.

"Ben," I said, prodding him. "Wake up. You're in trouble"

**BEN opened his eyes, stretched, and then heaved himself up reluctantly. I couldn't bear to meet his eyes.**

"Come on, they're waiting in the kitchen," I told him, and walked up the path, hoping that Ben was just behind.

P.C. Watson was propping up the fridge as we came in, but I realised, with sinking heart, that his usually friendly face looked quite stern and remote. He straightened himself up and eyed Ben up and down.

"Well, now, my lad," said the policeman. "What have you been up to? We've had complaints from several people at the end of the street and the postman, and . . ."

Ben looked long and hard at P.C. Watson, then he wagged his long tail, and jumped up to put his great, shaggy paws on P.C. Watson's chest.

Exchanging glances with Mum, I heaved a sigh of relief. That was all right, then. P.C. Watson was a dog lover after all. Ben can always tell.

So, in the end, as it was Ben's first offence, we got off with only a warning. But, from now on, that front gate is going to be kept tight shut. We can't risk a brush with the law a second time.

**THE END**

DANGER, MIN AT WORK!

EVER since she had left school, Min's hardest job had been keeping a job. One morning, Min started a new job on a farm.

Aa-aaah! This is better than working in a smoggy old town! Fresh milk and eggs, all this fresh air, and birds singing!

Farmer MacSpreader, was to be Min's new boss.
Are you the wee townie come here to work?
That's me, and I like it here, so I'll be working really hard to keep this job.

Oh, aye? It's hard work here . . . wet, mucky, and smelly at times.
That won't worry me—I'll just get on with the work.

Min was too eager.
Let me help—OOPS!

Look out!

Gurgle! Splut! S-sorry about that!
GURGLE
SPLUT
No need to worry about the eggs . . .

. . . you can pay for 'em out of your wages!
Thanks a bundle!

Take this hoe and weed the turnips in the far field.
Yes, farmer.

Later—
This is slow, boring work. If only I could think of a quick way of weeding turnips, Farmer MacSpreader might let me off paying for the eggs out of my wages!

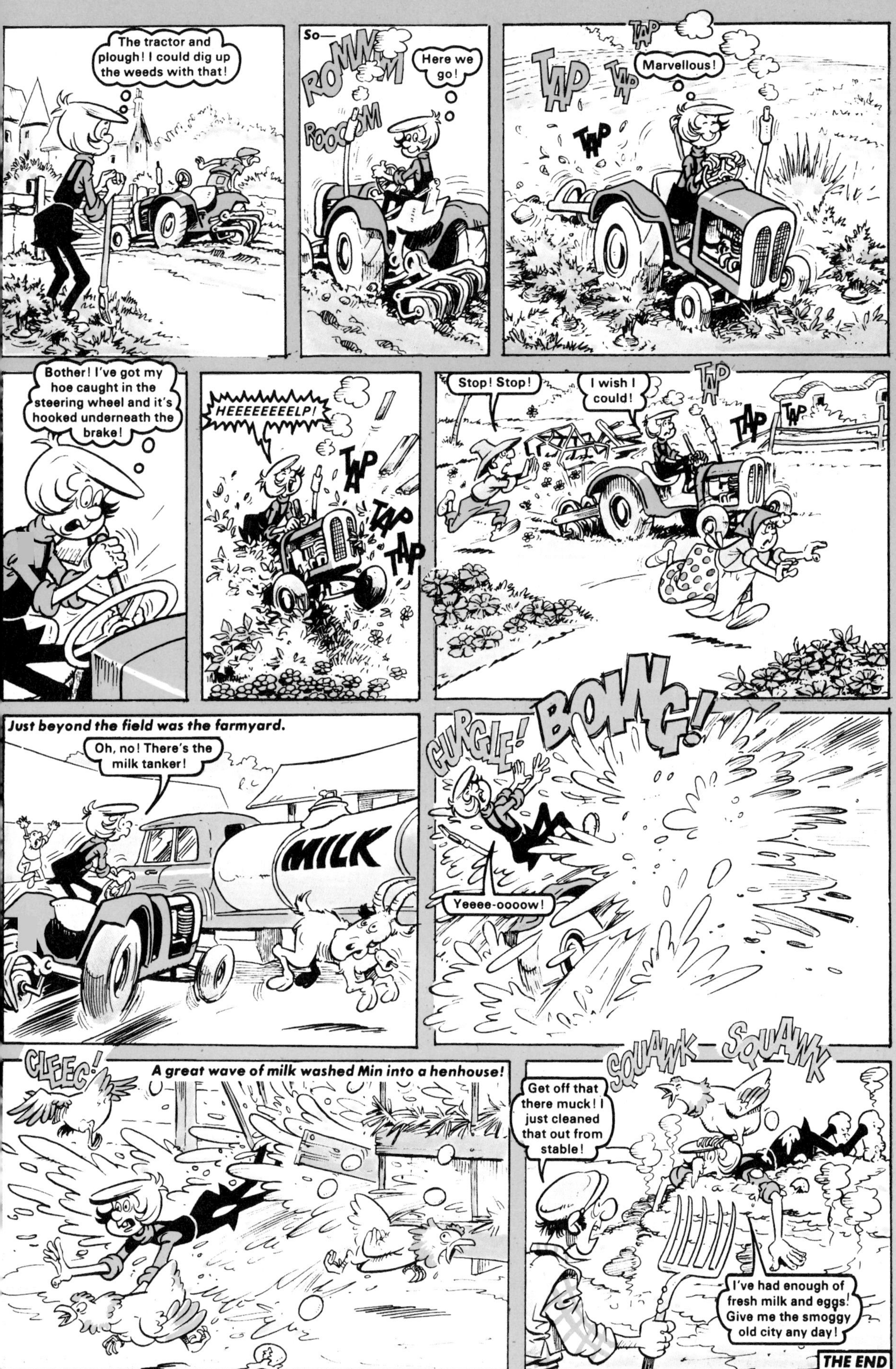
The tractor and plough! I could dig up the weeds with that!
So—
ROMMM
ROOOOM
Here we go!
TAP
TAP
TAP
Marvellous!
TAP
Bother! I've got my hoe caught in the steering wheel and it's hooked underneath the brake!
HEEEEEEEELP!
TAP
TAP
TAP
Stop! Stop!
I wish I could!
TAP
TAP
TAP
Just beyond the field was the farmyard.
Oh, no! There's the milk tanker!
MILK
GURGLE!
BOING!
Yeeee-oooow!
CLEEC!
A great wave of milk washed Min into a henhouse!
SQUAWK
SQUAWK
Get off that there muck! I just cleaned that out from stable!
I've had enough of fresh milk and eggs! Give me the smoggy old city any day!
THE END

# POOL FUN

HERE'S NUMBER ONE— A CHANNEL SWIM!

DID YOU LEARN TO SWIM THIS SUMMER? HERE ARE SOME WAYS OF HAVING FUN NOW THAT YOU'RE BACK AT THE LOCAL POOL.

THE ONLY DIFFERENCE IS— YOU DO IT IN YOUR OWN POOL, AND OVER A PERIOD OF MONTHS, RECORDING YOUR DISTANCES ON EACH POOL VISIT. A REAL CHANNEL SWIM IS 21 MILES. TRY TO BEAT YOUR FRIENDS!

AND HERE'S A NOVEL RACE. EACH SWIMMER BUTTS A BALLOON ACROSS, BUT MUSTN'T TOUCH IT WITH HANDS OR FEET!

FINALLY, TIE A HULA-HOOP TO A BRICK, AS YOU SEE HERE, AND PUT IT ON THE BOTTOM OF THE POOL (WITH PERMISH!) THEN PRACTISE DIVING OFF THE SIDE AND THROUGH THE HOOP. DON'T YOU THINK I'M CLEVER, BEING ABLE TO TALK UNDER WATER?

DON'T TRY ANYTHING, NATCH, THAT ISN'T WELL WITHIN YOUR CAPABILITIES.

YOU'LL FIND THIS SUPER PURSE VERY USEFUL, AND IT'S SO EASY TO MAKE. IT HAS TWO LARGE COMPARTMENTS, PLUS ONE SMALL ONE IN THE CENTRE FOR POSTAGE STAMPS. FIRST OF ALL, YOU NEED TWO PIECES OF SHEET PLASTIC CUT TO THE SIZES SHOWN BELOW.

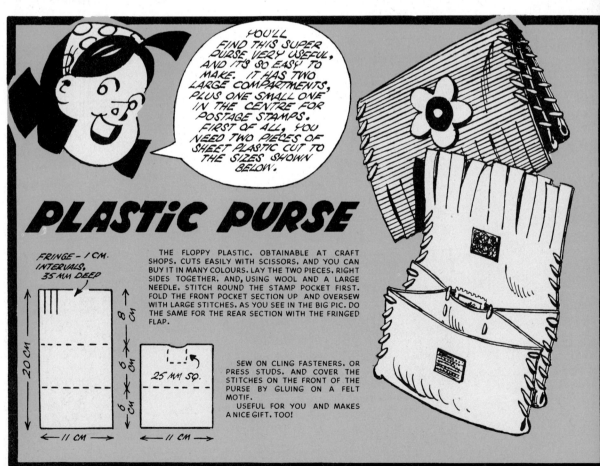

# PLASTIC PURSE

FRINGE – 1 CM. INTERVALS, 35 MM DEEP

20 CM

8 CM

6 CM

6 CM

← 11 CM →

25 MM SQ.

← 11 CM →

THE FLOPPY PLASTIC, OBTAINABLE AT CRAFT SHOPS, CUTS EASILY WITH SCISSORS, AND YOU CAN BUY IT IN MANY COLOURS. LAY THE TWO PIECES, RIGHT SIDES TOGETHER, AND, USING WOOL AND A LARGE NEEDLE, STITCH ROUND THE STAMP POCKET FIRST. FOLD THE FRONT POCKET SECTION UP AND OVERSEW WITH LARGE STITCHES, AS YOU SEE IN THE BIG PIC. DO THE SAME FOR THE REAR SECTION WITH THE FRINGED FLAP.

SEW ON CLING FASTENERS, OR PRESS STUDS, AND COVER THE STITCHES ON THE FRONT OF THE PURSE BY GLUING ON A FELT MOTIF.

USEFUL FOR YOU AND MAKES A NICE GIFT, TOO!

# Betty's Bloodhound Butler

BETTY JONES owned a bloodhound called Butler. There was something very special about her pet—he could talk, although only Betty could understand him.

Our neighbours' little girl, Susie, has a birthday today. I'm going to buy her a present and I know just what she wants.

Indeed, madam?

That cuddly toy dog. It's expensive, but Susie will love it!

As they came out of the shop—

We'll take the present straight to her house . . . no, wait—there's Susie herself, with her elder sister, Anne.

Hello, Susie. I've got a present for you. Happy birthday!

Say ' thank-you ', Susie.

I don't want it. I want that funny-looking doggy in the hat!

Susie!

Funny looking doggy in the hat? That young person is mocking me, madam!
Calm down, Butler. Susie's sister will sort things out.
Susie, you can't have Butler . . . he's Betty's dog.
It's my birthday and I want him!
Nice doggy! He's all mine now!
There's only one answer to this, Anne. I must get Butler away from Susie.
OK, Betty, leave the toy dog with me.
Never have I been so humiliated, madam!
Forget it, Butler! Just run!
Oh, no! Susie's following us! You'll have to hide, Butler!
SUPERMARKET
Madam, I cannot enter these premises, because . . .
NO DOGS
No time for arguments, Butler! Just hide— anywhere!
Susie's sister came along.
Betty, where's Susie?
Oh, she was following us, but now she's vanished!
Perhaps she ran after Butler. He went through that doorway.
Help me to find Susie, Betty.

But, inside a supermarket—
Who brought that dressed-up dog in here? Get him out!
Out! Out!
Eek!
Meanwhile—
Hey, Anne, here's Susie—in this pet shop!
If I can't have the funny doggy in the hat, then I'll have that puppy, please.
Annie came to fetch her little sister.
Sorry about that, sir. Susie doesn't realise you have to pay for things.
That's all right, miss. My own little daughter's just the same.
Nice, cuddly doggy! I want it!
Let go! It's not yours!
Tessa!
Susie!
Outside the shop—
There you are, Butler! We've a problem here—two squabbling little girls!
So I observe, madam—and your expensive present is liable to do some damage.
I can offer a solution, madam. That is, if the shop-keeper is agreeable.
I'm listening, Butler.
So—
Look, sir, suppose your daughter keeps the cuddly toy and Susie has this puppy?
That's a good idea! It's Tessa's birthday soon.
Well done, Butler! Peace and quiet at last!
Quite so, madam. Good work for a "funny-looking doggy," don't you agree?
THE END

# THE BLACK DOG

*LINDA LLOYD, the seventh child of a seventh child, inherited from her Highland ancestors a sixth sense that enabled her to see things invisible to ordinary eyes. She helped her uncle—a member of the Society for Psychical Research—to investigate ghosts and haunted houses.*

*One day, a woman in great distress called on the professor.*

Calm yourself, Mrs Brown, and tell us all about it.
Drink this tea, and you'll feel better.
It's about my son, Toby . . .

*Mrs Brown told of how, ever since Toby had been a toddler, he had wanted a dog, but she had always said the house was too small. Then he had invented an imaginary, big, black dog, and used to talk to this dog day and night.*

Then, last week I saw it going into Toby's room! But when I went to look for it, it wasn't there! No-one else has seen it!

I think this is a case for you, Linda. Will you go with Mrs Brown and see if you can help her?
Of course, Uncle.

Later, at Mrs Brown's home—
You go in and have a look round while I fetch Toby from a neighbour. He hasn't any friends of his own age, I'm afraid.

Linda searched the house.
This must be Toby's room. There's no sign of any dog.

Just then, Toby came in.
What are you doing in my room?
Hello, Toby. I came to see your dog.

Suddenly Linda saw the dog.
It's unbelievable!
Here, Big Dog. Come on—let's play.

Big Dog is my friend— my very best friend.
Yes, Toby.
And your only friend, I'll bet.

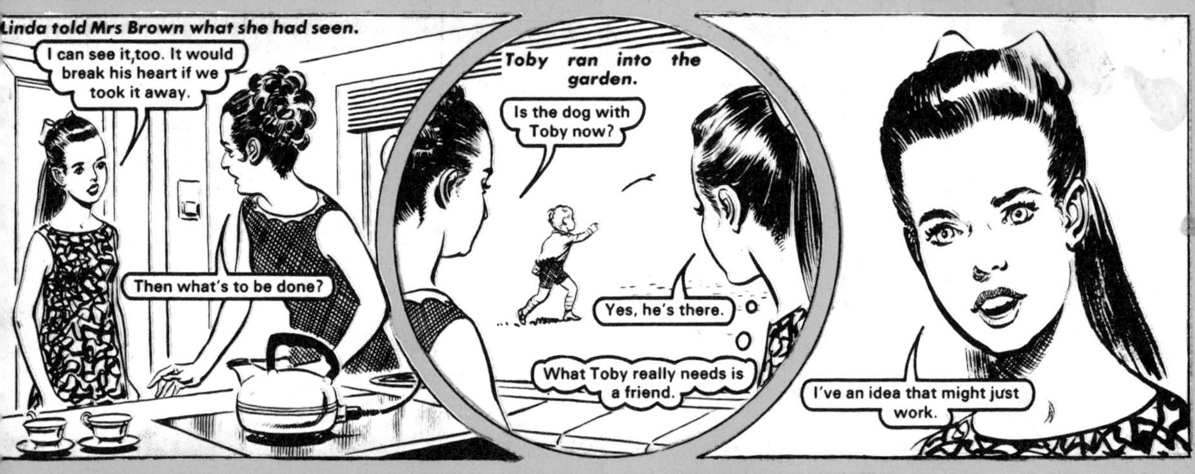
Linda told Mrs Brown what she had seen.
I can see it, too. It would break his heart if we took it away.
Then what's to be done?
Toby ran into the garden.
Is the dog with Toby now?
Yes, he's there.
What Toby really needs is a friend.
I've an idea that might just work.

Linda went to a pet shop.
I'll have this one, please.

Linda took the puppy up to Toby's room.
I've brought you a present, Toby.
For me? He's lovely! But what will Big Dog say?

Big Dog doesn't belong here. You know that, Toby. You must tell him he can go home now.
All right. Goodbye, Big Dog. Time to go home.

The dog disappeared.
Big Dog has gone home now, Toby. Promise you won't call him back?
I promise. I've got a real dog now!

Mrs Brown came in.
See my real dog, Mum? I'm going to call him Black, 'cos he's black all over.
Thank you, Linda!
Don't worry any more, Mrs Brown. I don't think Big Dog will be back.
THE END

# PONY TALES

ALWAYS TALK SOFTLY TO A PONY WHEN YOU FIRST APPROACH HIM, SAMANTHA, AS IT REASSURES HIM.

IT DOESN'T MATTER **WHAT** YOU SAY, JUST CALLING HIS NAME...

...SAYING HOW NICE HE LOOKS, ASKING HIM HOW HE IS TODAY, OR...

**...GET OFF MY FOOT!**

IF YOU HAVE A HANG-UP ABOUT PONIES, OR IF ONE OF YOUR FRIENDS HAS, THIS IS JUST THE THING!

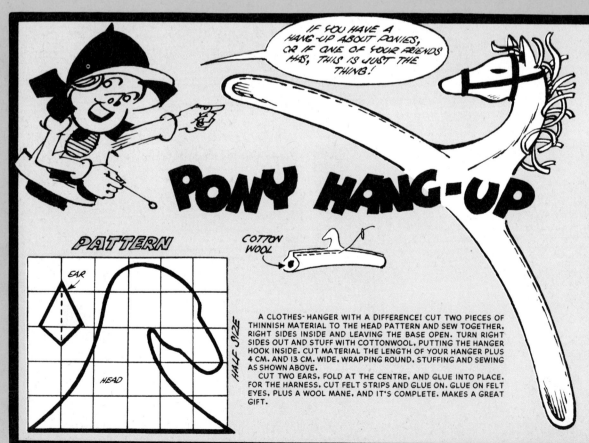

# PONY HANG-UP

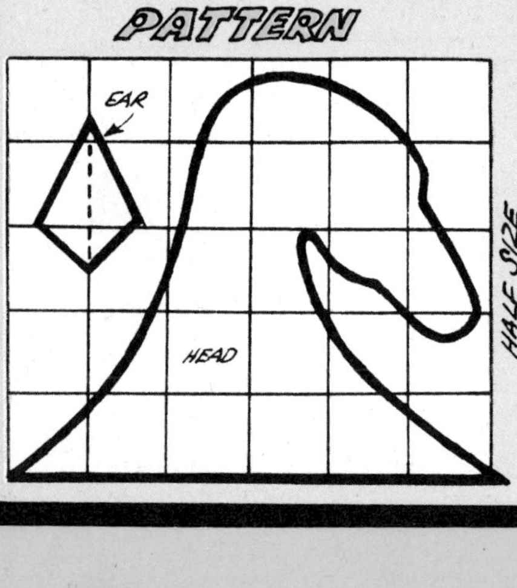

PATTERN

EAR

HEAD

HALF SIZE

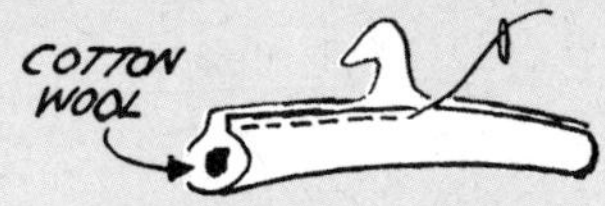

COTTON WOOL

A CLOTHES-HANGER WITH A DIFFERENCE! CUT TWO PIECES OF THINNISH MATERIAL TO THE HEAD PATTERN AND SEW TOGETHER, RIGHT SIDES INSIDE AND LEAVING THE BASE OPEN. TURN RIGHT SIDES OUT AND STUFF WITH COTTONWOOL, PUTTING THE HANGER HOOK INSIDE. CUT MATERIAL THE LENGTH OF YOUR HANGER PLUS 4 CM. AND 13 CM. WIDE, WRAPPING ROUND, STUFFING AND SEWING AS SHOWN ABOVE.

CUT TWO EARS, FOLD AT THE CENTRE, AND GLUE INTO PLACE. FOR THE HARNESS, CUT FELT STRIPS AND GLUE ON. GLUE ON FELT EYES, PLUS A WOOL MANE, AND IT'S COMPLETE. MAKES A GREAT GIFT.

PHOTO FINISH
ONLY £1
JUNE SIMONS had never been able to afford a camera of her own so, when she saw one in the window of the local junk shop, she didn't hesitate.
It's a bargain, miss. One of the very first instant picture cameras. There you are—it's already got some film in it. Just take a snap and pull out the picture.
Thanks!
hurried home to try
ut her purchase.
I'll try photographing this vase. Couldn't be simpler to operate.
Super! I wonder if it takes as good pictures outside. I'll have a walk down the road.

The local church was famed for its architecture.
This should make a good shot.

And it did.
Better than ever! I must show this to Mum. She'll be home from work by now.

June's mother had had an unpleasant surprise.
Mum! I've got . . . oh, what's happened?
Great-grandmother's vase. The draught must have blown it over and it's smashed.

Just as well I took the picture. At least we have something to remember it by.

Shortly afterwards, June's father arrived home.
Dad, I bought a camera and . . .
Never mind that just now! Come and see what I have outside!

The firm's given me a new car!
It's great, Dad! Let me get a picture of it!

Good photo, isn't it? The camera only cost a pound, too.
Next morning in the local paper—
That's the church I photographed yesterday! What a terrible thing to happen!
RUNAWAY LORRY DAMAGES CHURCH

houghtfully, June went out into the garden.
There's something strange happening, if only I can figure it out. Oh . . . the summer house.

It took Dad all spring to build it. He'd like a picture of it.

*Just then, June's father arrived home in a taxi.*

Dad! What happened?

A bit of an accident with the car, June.

*In the house—*

Mum'll be back from shopping soon. How did it happen?

Some joker jumped the traffic lights at the junction and rammed me in the side.

I was lucky to escape more serious injury but the car will be off the road for a few weeks.

It's ridiculous, but I can't help feeling . . .

*At that moment, June's mother came in with a neighbour's child.*

Good gracious! What's happened? Here, June, look after Jimmy Green. His mother will be round later.

Come on, Jimmy—let's go into the garden.

Looks as if there's a storm blowing up. We'd better go up to my room.
OK, June.

oon as they went upstairs—
The summer house! I knew it! It's the camera! Everything I've snapped has come to harm!
Oo! Nice camera!

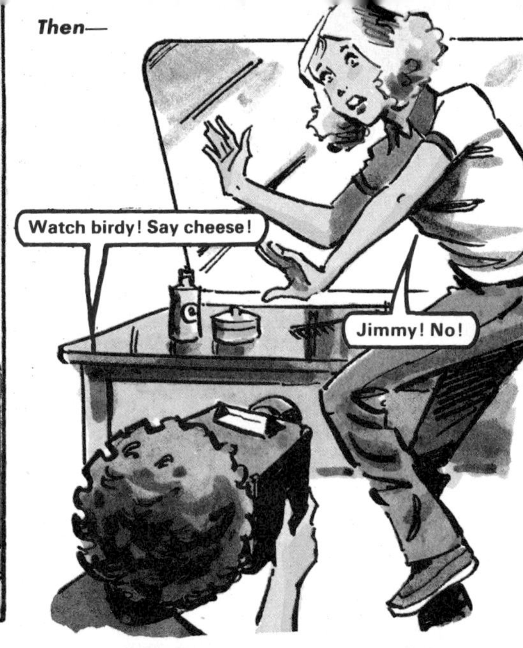
Then—
Watch birdy! Say cheese!
Jimmy! No!

desperation, June snatched the camera and ran towards the town.

This hateful thing! I'll throw it over that junk dealer's wall! It's evil!

But the wet pavement was slippery.
Yow!

The camera's broken . . . ruined . . . I don't understand! I'm sure that I was intended to fall nder that truck, since I was the subject of the last photo! I must see the last photograph!

It missed me, and photographed itself in the mirror. I see! Since the camera caused harm to everything it photographed, its fate was sealed from the moment it took a photograph of itself!
THE END

# HOW TO DRAW YOUR OWN

# FARMYARD FAMILY

All you have to do is follow the instructions on the opposite page to learn how to draw the animals. Copy the farmyard shown here, or design your own.

**Everything has been simplified into shapes that build up to make the finished drawing. Red lines show the new shape to be added at each stage. Use a pencil, so that you can rub out any mistakes.**

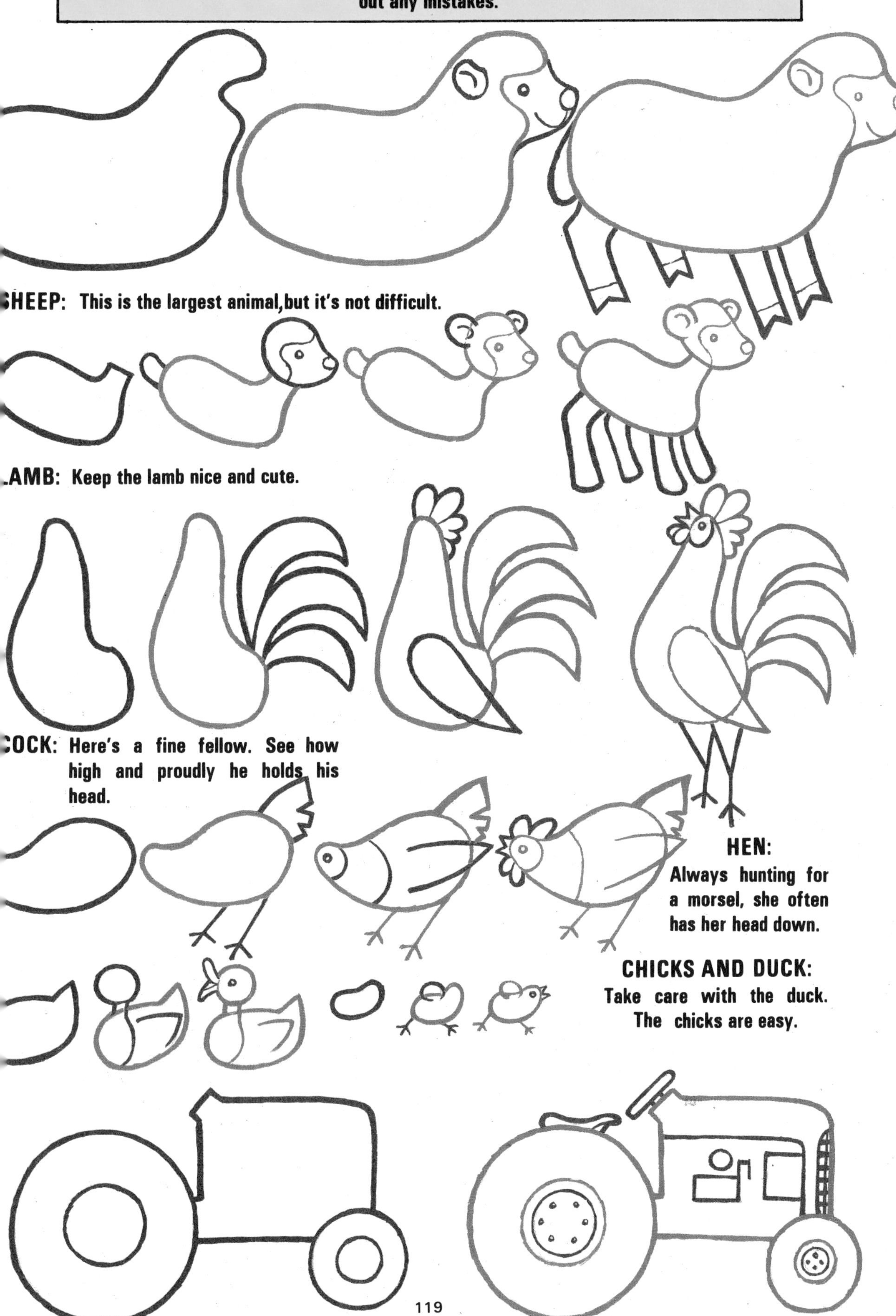

HEEP: This is the largest animal, but it's not difficult.
AMB: Keep the lamb nice and cute.
OCK: Here's a fine fellow. See how high and proudly he holds his head.
HEN:
Always hunting for a morsel, she often has her head down.
CHICKS AND DUCK:
Take care with the duck. The chicks are easy.

Reluctant Heroine
FRANCES DOYLE'S parents took her to Carmouth every year for their fortnight's holiday—and Frances was bored stiff with the place.
Same old room, same old guest house, same old boring beach—it's a wonder Mum and Dad didn't pack my bucket and spade this year!
Frances' parents entered with three strangers.
Frances, meet Doris and Jack Thomas, and their son, Keith. They're staying here this year.
Keith looks dishy!
Our folks seem to have hit it off, Frances. How about showing me around the town tomorrow?
Call me Fran. I'd love to—though it isn't exactly the Riviera!
Next day—
This is fun—but I prefer to be outdoors. How about a swim tomorrow, if it's fine?
Er—sure, K
Suits m
So—
Underwater swimming—that's the sport, Fran. Here, I've brought a spare mask and flippers for you.
No! I couldn't—er—I'm not that keen.

I thought you'd enjoy it, but suit yourself!
There he goes. I should have told him I'm terrified of being underwater.
Later—
That was great, Fran. Why didn't you come, too? I know you can swim. You could have picked it up easily.
Oh, don't keep on about your silly old diving! I'm hungry, and it's time for lunch at the guest house!
In the guest house—
I discovered a hidden cave out at the point last year. Would you like to walk out there and explore it?
Sure, sounds fine—as long as you don't lose your temper again!
After lunch—
Sorry I was so rude earlier, Keith. It's just that, when I was a toddler, somebody pushed me into a pool and I nearly drowned. Since then, I've had a fear of being underwater.

Why didn't you tell me before? Maybe I could help you to get over this phobia, Fran.
Thanks, but I doubt if anybody could.
Later—
This is the spot. You can just see the cave entrance under the cliffs here. We'll need our torches.
It's a bit narrow, isn't it?
The tunnel opens out soon.
Wow! Some cave, Fran!
FRAN-AN-AN.
Good echo, too!
Hey, Fran! Looks like the entrance to an inner cave.
So it does. Let's go through.
There's light coming from the cave roof. That must lead to the cliff top.
Don't try to climb it, Keith. Le
explore this cave while we're h

Some time later—
We'd best be heading back, now. Come on, Fran.
But when they reached the outer cave—
Oh, no! The tide's come in and the entrance is underwater!
We'll go back to the inner cave. We'll be safe there as it's above the high-water mark.
Soon afterwards—
You know, I reckon I *could* climb up there to the cliff top. Could you give me a hand?
Careful, Keith. It looks dangerous.
Better than hanging about here for hours with our parents worrying. I'll be fine once I reach that ledge . . .
Made it! Now I'll be up in no time.
Look out!

Suddenly, the slab Keith was holding gave way.
Aaah!
Are you badly hurt?
It's my leg, Fran! I can't—aah—can't move it! I think it's broken!
You need medical attention urgently—and there's only one way out of here!
No, Fran! Don't risk it! I'll be fine!
But Fran was determined.
Come back, Fran!
The entrance is just ahead. Here goes!
The passageway seems even narrower now it's filled with water.

surge of the incoming tide forced
an's head against the tunnel wall.

Ooh! I must go on!

After what seemed a very long time—

I'm through! I can see a man on the beach!

Soon, Fran was gasping out her story.
... and he's trapped in the cave with a broken leg! We must hurry!
I know the spot. Don't worry, my dear. I'll direct the rescue service to that hole in the cliff top. We'll soon have him out.

Next day, in the cottage hospital —

How are you, Keith?

Fine, thanks to you. An hour after you left, I was hoisted to the surface —after a doctor had given me a pain-killing injection.

I never thought you'd make it through that tunnel, though. It must have taken a lot of courage.

Well, you *did* say you could cure me of my fear of underwater swimming—but you might have chosen a less dramatic way of doing it!

**THE END.**

Siamese Cat
Blackbir
Artichoke Flo
Cairngorm, Scotland